HILL SPIRITS IV

An Anthology by writers
of Northumberland County

Edited by
Felicity Sidnell Reid
Gwynn Scheltema
Susan Statham

Published by Blue Denim Press Inc.
Cover design: Robert Scozzari
Copy editor: Christopher Cameron
Published in Canada
ISBN 978-1-927882-49-8

Canadian Cataloguing in Publication Data
Title: Hill Spirits : an anthology by writers of Northumberland County.
Names: Sidnell Reid, Felicity, 1936- editor. | Scheltema, Gwynn, 1954- editor. | Statham, Susan,
  1951- editor.
Description: First edition. | Volume IV edited by Felicity Sidnell Reid, Gwynn Scheltema, Susan Statham.
Identifiers: Canadiana (print) 20129053813 | Canadiana (ebook) 20129053821 | ISBN 9781927882498 (v.
  4 ; softcover) | ISBN 9781927882504 (v. 4 ; Kindle) | ISBN 9781927882511 (v. 4 ; EPUB)
Subjects: CSH: Canadian literature (English)—Ontario—Northumberland. | CSH: Canadian literature
  (English)—21st century.
Classification: LCC PS8255.O5 H55 2012 | DDC C810.8/0971357—dc23

"The unread story is not a story; it is little black marks on wood pulp.
The reader, reading it, makes it live: a live thing, a story."
— Ursula K. Le Guin, *Dancing at the Edge of the World*

Welcome

Welcome to *Hill Spirits IV*!

In 2019, Spirit of the Hills Arts Association marks its twentieth anniversary. The association's membership includes over 160 artists, who live in all parts of Northumberland and surrounding counties and work in a wide variety of fields.

The launch of *Hill Spirits IV* is part of our second Festival of the Arts, October 24 to 26, 2019. The festival brings our members together to work cooperatively on a programme which showcases the talents of our visual artists, artisans and photographers, our playwrights, poets, short story and non-fiction writers, as well as the many musicians, dancers, multi-media artists and actors from our community.

The theme chosen for the festival is "Sharing Across the Arts," and writers and illustrators were asked to investigate the concept of sharing and its positive and negative connotations when they submitted items to the anthology. Authors took the opportunity to write on a great variety of topics and in many different styles so that once again this new *Hill Spirits* anthology contains something for everyone. Also included in the anthology are the winners of the festival's poetry and short prose contests.

The editors thank the writers and artists who submitted their work and are especially grateful to Christopher Cameron for his careful copy editing.

We hope you enjoy *Hill Spirits IV*!

The Editors:

Felicity Sidnell Reid

Gwynn Scheltema

Susan Statham

Table of Contents

CONTRIBUTORS

Michael Croucher

TIME RIVER

Archie and Ted were best friends but they bickered constantly. Archie liked talking, and he loved telling whoppers. Ted was a nag. He'd pestered Archie for over twenty years to take him to his secret fishing spot.

One day after Archie's car had been repossessed, the pestering paid off. Archie agreed to share the location if Ted drove. Ted was thrilled to be going and said he'd drive, even pay for the gas, as long as Archie laid off his crazy stories. He hated them. They gave him the creeps.

They left the truck in a clearing off a county road thirty-five miles from home, then walked along a rough path that started behind a copse of trees. It took twenty minutes to reach the river and the bend where it turned to the west.

Archie breathed deeply, sighed, and pulled one of two flasks from his pocket. "Ah yes, here it is Teddy. My fisherman's paradise." He took two sips from the flask and picked up his fishing rod.

His reel buzzed. The green popper cut through the air and flopped down near a cluster of lily pads. Within seconds the popper bounced lightly on the surface and then submerged into a dark swirl. The rod bowed and vibrated with urgent tugs. Archie chuckled. He snapped the tip up sharply to set the hook and leaned out with the rod high to bring the fish through an underwater maze of long-dead branches to shore. Once the hook was removed from his first catch of the day, a smallmouth bass, he released it into the river.

Archie looked at Ted. He'd also landed a fish on his first cast. This promised to be a bountiful day of fishing; Archie figured Ted would be wetting himself with glee, maybe receptive to some chatter. He glanced towards the far bank and the location of his most outrageous claim, then cast the popper in that direction, a little further upstream, letting it drift to the spot.

Ted raised his flask, took a sip and nodded. "Damned beautiful! This is what it's all about. Thanks for bringing me. What a great start. This might be as good as you said."

"I love it here, Teddy. Lots more fish to come." Archie pointed to where his popper was submerging again. "And you know, it was right there it happened. At the bend of the river, near that bank and the big boulder. It was as real and as solid as the rock itself."

"Oh, Jesus wept. Please don't spoil the day with crap stories. Especially that one. I've heard it enough."

Archie took another drink. He wiped his lips on the back of his sleeve. "I tell you, there was a lean-to over there. Two guys carrying muskets and bundles of pelts went to it from a canoe. A birch-bark; they looked just like them courier de bois guys in the history books."

"Horse crap. You drink too much. Especially when you fish," said Ted.

Archie shrugged. "As God is my judge, bud, this is a magical place—on a very strange river."

"Archie, I came up here to fish. One more word about that stupid story or any other story, I'll take my truck and leave your drunken ass here."

"You wouldn't go, Teddy. Hell, we could both land twenty or more. The day is young. Enjoy the fishing." He did a little jig. "Oh yeah. A magical place."

"Son of a bitch. Put a sock in it." Ted picked up his gear and moved thirty paces down the bank. He knew Archie wouldn't shout; loud noises might scare off the fish.

They fished for hours. Ted stayed downstream from Archie, happy not to hear more about those mystery trappers. Both men lost count of their catches, but it was an amazing day of fishing. The fish had all been released to the river. Except for two. Ted put those on an aluminum stringer for his supper. He anchored the stringer to its spike and submerged it in the river.

When he figured it was time to go, Ted picked up the stringer. He walked back to Archie, his fish by his side, the stringer dripping and clinking with his steps.

Archie looked at him. "We don't keep any of our catch."

Ted shook his head. "I always eat some of my bloody catch, and I'll have these tonight. Don't give a shit what you say." He turned away from Archie. "Come on, it's time to head back."

"No way. Just half an hour more. The fishing is too good."

Ted shrugged, laid the stringer on a patch of grass and splashed it with river water. He watched his bass flop around, picked up his rod, and cast upstream. He landed another big bass. Already happy with the day and content that he had supper on the stringer, he released it. Both men fished on and caught even more. Eventually, the sun slipped below the tree tops, the air stilled, and mosquitoes started to find them. The ripple on the river gave way to a glassy stillness. A thick mist built to a fog along the banks. They put on their jackets and rounded up their gear.

Ted retrieved his stringer and supper. "Terrific day, Arch. Let's head home." He started towards the path.

"Wait up, Teddy. Something's happening." Archie pointed to the far bank.

Through the thickening fog, at the turn of the river, a canoe appeared. It glided slowly in front of them, sitting low in the water, weighed down. Two men, pelts piled between them, sat in the canoe. Several ancient muskets rested against the pile of pelts. As their paddles sliced into the river powerfully and quietly, the canoe turned and made its final push to the big boulder.

Archie's face lit up. He skipped towards the river and hollered. "Hellooo, there!"

Ted gasped. He dove behind a tree.

Archie laughed. "It's just like the other times. Don't worry, bud. They can't see or hear us."

"Don't talk. Just shut up," whispered Ted. He was flat on his belly and crawling to the path. "They're armed for Christ's sake."

"Relax, you old shit. We're in the same place as them, just at a different time." Archie sucked the remaining drops from his second flask.

"Stop talking that bullshit, Archie." Ted stood and ran up the path. He dropped his stringer into a live-fish box in the bed of the truck and scrambled into the cab. Archie reluctantly climbed aboard a few minutes later.

Ted drove onto the county road. A quarter of a mile south, he pulled into a track off the shoulder. "We'd better sleep it off, Archie."

After a long nap, they drove home. Neither man spoke until Ted turned the truck into their shared gravel lane.

"I'm glad you came, Teddy. Now you can vouch for my story," said Archie.

"No. I won't vouch for anything. Nothing happened. Not a goddamned thing. I'm never going back to that place, Arch. Screw you. You'll have to get another ride or just walk."

Teddy got out and reached into the live-fish box for his supper. He lifted out his stringer, looked at it in amazement and then at Archie in disbelief. "Jesus…What the—?"

Archie grinned and clapped his hands. "Told you, Teddy. No sense in keeping them."

Ted walked to his front door cursing. He stopped just before he reached his house, shuddered, and flung the empty stringer onto his lawn.

Wally Keeler

RAINBOW TROUT

It has only primal need
to feed and breed
so it gulps
the hook dressed in wormdrag
piercing its gill
like a gothic earring
mouthful of pain
it flees
shocks my slack line
I jerk it back
dig it in deeper

"Oh it's a fighter!"

I thrill
it thrashes
in the cool
in the clear
splinters of sunlight
in the splash
in the thrash
in the thrust
of slender steel
in soft yielding gill
its community of peers
scatter with skittish fears

"Oh it's a fighter!"

I play it
enjoy the luxury of several runs-for-its-life
spinning spool
dizzy with escape
I jerk it back
with jackboot ferocity
play it to the end

This is sport
splashing, thrashing
the will to survive
versus
the will to kill, eat
the destiny of doom
net scoop into liquid sky
light diamonds dripping
off its muscles
of swim and swoop
in the cool
in the clear

I admire the smooth rainbow sinew
unhooking indelicately
plunking without dignity
into the bucket
end of the rainbow
gasping captured colleagues
wounded mouths
puckering pain

Single swipe throat cut
blade tip in orifice
spilling slippery guts
into the clear
into the cold
thumbs massaging separating
conglomeration of organs
amputation of fins

Seagull swoops and swipes
guts glistening blood and sun
from the clear
from the cool
to the nest
for the chicks

Pan prep
s I z z z z z l e
children clamour to the fireside
bubbles of exuberance, chatter, chirp, laughter
as their small teeth sink
into the lemon succulence
of well-done death.

Antony Di Nardo

WATER

Drink from my cup and I'll share the lake with you.
I'll bring you bodies of water, bottles and ponds,
rivers and waterways between.

I'll give you oceans vast, endless and impenetrable,
philosophies of water dear and close to me.
Nearby canals.
The lake down the street.
The pond behind the house.
A river I return to and share the course it follows.
Aquifers I draw from beneath my feet.
Snowflakes at 900 metres.

Kind water. Green or blue. Deep or shallow.
Water, nonetheless.
Nevertheless,
I need it close to me.
Nearby.
Close to where I share a cup with you.

We'll drink a gallon, sip and slurp.
We'll fill our heads to the brim.

A tin cup coming straight up dripping wet from the belly of the well.
That kind of water too.

Right as rain.
Cool as driven snow.

Ice and water.
Ice in chunks and sides of ice.
Ice that dignifies its source.

I know of an island people lovely as an iceberg.
And of snow-feathers.
Crystals.
And watery dew on a mountain meadow.

Musical Harmony of Friends by Dania Madera-Lerman

Cynthia Reyes

THE BEACH

Alicia had always known she'd stay in Lakeridge.

Her brother and sister had gone to university in Toronto and stayed there, but she had returned home right after completing her nursing studies.

She lived in the family home on Lakeview Road. A short walk from the beach, the two-storey brick house and perennial garden drew admiring glances, especially in summer. It had been passed down through the generations, from Alicia's grandparents to her parents, then to her and Ron thirty years ago.

Alicia knew every part of this town.

As if there was a map in her mind, she could close her eyes and see the buildings and sidewalks on almost every street.

The grocery store on Smith Avenue: when they were ten, she and Julie-Ann rode their bikes to buy popsicles there.

The children's clothing store on Main Street: their clothes were always bought there, at a discount, because her mother was the manager.

St. Michael's, the grand church on Clearview Street: she and her siblings were all baptized there, and years later Alicia and Ron got married there. Their son and daughter were baptized there too.

Her mind's eye returned to her own street, and to its farthest point south, Lake Ontario. The glistening water pulled at her like a magnet.

How do people live away from the water? she wondered.

The lake, the endless horizon, the beach, the warm sand between her toes—all of it was home.

Alicia's mind went back to the Saturday afternoons of her childhood. There they were, her whole family, walking along the beach.

Well, the parents walked, but she and her sister and brother always ran. Three children in brightly coloured bathing suits, laughing, running and calling to each other, plastic buckets and shovels in hand.

She smiled.

She had felt free and secure in this town where she knew almost everyone she saw.

Until now.

***

Sadia and Imad had good jobs in Pakistan—she a bank manager, he an IT technician. They owned a modest home, a short walk from where her parents lived.

Between the two houses, their lives bustled with the comings and goings of extended families and friends. Otherwise, it was a simple life in their harbourside city with its smell of seawater, the long sandy beach, and the glittering ocean.

Sadia and Imad had dreams for their children, six-year-old Irshaad and three-year-old Hamza. But they worried about the country's political and economic instability.

One day, a letter came from her brother, Omer, who lived in a town just east of Toronto.

"You really should move to Canada," his letter said. "The schools are good and the neighbourhoods are safe. You can live with us till you're fully settled. You'll like it."

The thought of a better future for the children took root in Sadia's mind. Imad wasn't sure. His job was secure; he knew where he stood. And he loved their seaside town. Sadia, though, wanted them to move to Canada. "The children will have much better opportunities there," she repeated.

"You're sure about this?" he asked. "Uprooting everyone, giving up everything, leaving our families behind?"

"Yes, but we'll make a new life in Canada," she countered. "We'll live with Omer and Sana, save money and buy our own home. Plus," she added, smiling, "with so many of us there, our relatives will have twice the reason to visit."

Sadia eventually got her way. She often did. Imad gave in, deciding to trust her judgment.

***

When they landed at Pearson airport, the warm embraces from Sadia's brother and sister-in-law Sana and the shy smiles from their young son Arsh and daughter Arzoo helped temper the bitter January cold.

Snow was piled high on both sides of the road. The four new arrivals gaped at the sight.

The families got along well. The children were almost the same ages and sometimes squabbled, as children do. But there had been very few arguments between the adults.

Three years later, they were still living in the basement. It was cramped, but everyone knew the situation was temporary. Sadia and Imad were saving for a down payment on their own home. It would be nearby, of course; they wanted to stay close.

In their very first year they started a summer tradition, and three years later they still kept it up. Almost every Sunday, the two families packed a picnic, loads of toys, and a charcoal barbecue, and piled into Omer's grey minivan, heading to a beach an hour east of town.

***

Alicia's daughter and son-in-law often brought their two young sons to visit on summer weekends. Alicia kept a supply of sun-block, beach towels, shovels and buckets—yellow and blue plastic buckets—ready for them.

Sometimes her daughter and son-in-law accompanied the children, but often it was Alicia who took them to the nearby beach while the parents visited local friends.

They went twice: once on Saturday afternoon, once on Sunday. The kids used the buckets to fetch water from the lake, the shovels to dig sand and make pretend-castles. Then, their castles built, bodies covered in sand, they went back into the water, splashing themselves and each other, shouting and laughing. Sometimes they bent to pick up a funny-looking shell or a piece of coloured glass.

It was a replay of Alicia's own childhood. The beach, the streets, her home—it was all a precious legacy that Alicia had inherited and was now sharing with her daughter's children.

***

When Sadia looked out over the water to where the lake met the horizon, she imagined their hometown somewhere just beyond. She missed her family. She missed her seaside town.

But Canada was home now. They were lucky to live here, lucky to have a beautiful white-sand beach within driving distance.

Imad glanced at his wife as they strolled along the beach, the children running ahead. Sadia's brown skin glowed, her long dark hair shone in the sunlight. She radiated contentment. And when she smiled at their children or at him, it still made him weak in the knees. Imad wasn't a tall man, only five feet nine. But standing beside his petite wife, he felt like a giant. He felt protective toward her.

He had secured a job several months after his arrival: a junior role in the IT department of an insurance company, for which he was recommended by a friend of his brother-in-law. Canada wasn't that different from their homeland, he realized; who you knew mattered here too.

Sadia secured an even more junior role than his—in a bank—but she accepted it without complaint.

"It'll help towards the down payment," she said. "And I'll have some security."

Imad smiled as they walked on the beach. *We're so lucky,* he thought. *There are immigrants with PhDs driving cabs in Toronto.*

"Why are you smiling?" Sadia, who had seen his face change expression, asked.

"I was remembering how much I resisted coming to Canada," he said. "More than you know. I didn't want to come."

"And now?"

"Now I realize how blessed we are."

They looked at each other for a long moment. Sadia's eyes misted with gratitude.

That was when they heard a shout.

"That's my bucket!" a child's voice yelled.

"No, it's mine!" shouted another voice. Their son's.

A woman, fiftyish, hurried to where the children stood. "Give it to me," she told their son. "Right this minute!"

He clutched his bucket, frightened. "It's mine," he repeated.

The woman started to yank the bucket from the child.

"Wait!" Sadia said, walking quickly towards them. She inspected the yellow bucket. "This is my son's bucket," she said firmly.

"How do you know?" the woman demanded. With short, light-brown hair and an attractive face, she would have been lovely if she hadn't looked so angry.

Imad intervened. "It has a small crack on the side." He examined the bucket. "See?" he held it up to the woman. "It's ours."

The woman frowned, then turned away. "Come, sweeties," she told the two children on either side of her, reaching for their hands and walking away. "These people! I don't know why they keep crowding our beach."

Sadia bent and hugged her son. "It's okay, dear," she whispered, stroking his hair.

But her heart hurt. *These people*, she thought.

It had amazed her at first: Toronto was said to be the most multiracial city on the earth, but here, a short drive away, all the local people were white. Until now, her family had never felt rejected, never insulted. Yes, there had been a few strange looks from some of the white people on the beach. She had dismissed those looks as curiosity.

Now, for the first time, she realized she was one of *these people*. What did it mean?

"Give me a minute," she told Imad and rushed away before he could stop her.

Sadia hurried after the woman and children as they crossed the grass toward the street. "Excuse me," she called. "May I speak with you?"

The woman turned, looking confused. "Who? Me?"

"Yes, please. Could I have a word with you?"

The woman hesitated. "What about?"

"Do you live here in this town?" Sadia asked politely.

"All my life," the woman answered.

"My family and I live not far from here," Sadia said. "We love your beach."

"So do we," the woman answered abruptly.

"My name is Sadia. May I ask…what's yours?"

"Alicia," the woman answered. "Why do you want to know?"

"I want to say thank you, Miss Alicia."

"For what?"

"For allowing us to share your beach. It's a blessing to have a beach like this."

"Well, we don't have a choice," Alicia answered. She still did not smile, though she seemed slightly less hostile. "Anyone can come here."

"But not everyone has to like our coming here, Miss Alicia."

"Please, just 'Alicia' is fine."

"I'm sorry you don't like us coming to your beach, Alicia," Sadia said softly. "I'm sorry."

Ten minutes earlier, Alicia would have asked: "Then why don't you go somewhere else? Why *our* beach?" Instead she said, "I don't think…I don't think people are opposed to your coming here. It's just…it's just…it used to be *our* beach. We've worked so hard to keep it maintained. Now there are so many…"

Alicia paused, searching for the right word. "There are so many *tourists* here in the summer. We can't even get a spot to spread our picnic blankets unless we get here at dawn. There are just so many of you coming here."

Sadia swallowed hard. "You feel crowded out?" she asked.

"Honestly?" Alicia asked.

Sadia nodded.

Alicia paused, as if weighing her words. "Yes, we do. If we seem unfriendly at times, that's why. We pay taxes to take care of the town and the beach area, and we look forward to the weekends. But we can't use our beach freely any more. It's always crowded."

"With tourists like us," Sadia answered, looking into Alicia's eyes. "Thank you for being honest, Alicia. It's just that we miss our beach back home. Coming here reminds us a little of…home…" Her voice trailed off.

"It's okay," said Alicia. Her tone softened a little as she added, "It's not personal."

They parted, Alicia and Sadia heading in different directions, each unsettled by the encounter.

Sadia was shocked by what she'd done. Whatever had made her run after the woman? She walked toward her husband, wondering how much to tell him about the conversation. Would he want them to stop coming to the beach?

***

Alicia and her grandsons returned home. Her thoughts returned to the woman on the beach. Alicia had to give her credit: she had run after her, had tried to understand.

"A penny for your thoughts," Ron said as they lay awake that night. He listened attentively as she explained what happened.

"I still can't believe I nearly yanked the bucket from the kid," Alicia confessed.

"No," said Ron. "Not like you at all."

"They overwhelm me at times," she said. "All these…people."

"What if we were in their places?" Ron asked.

"Hmm," Alicia said after a pause. "The woman called the beach a 'blessing.' Said it reminds them of home."

"What will you do if you see her again?" Ron asked.

"Well," Alicia said slowly. "I'll…I'll probably approach her this time."

***

The children were tucked in. Sadia and Imad sat up in bed, scrolling through cell-phone photos from the beach. They'd post some on Facebook for relatives back home to see.

But the incident had surprised and rattled them. "We're obviously upsetting some people," Sadia said. "Should we stop going?"

Imad was silent, thinking. "Let's talk to Omer and Sana about it tomorrow," he said. He turned off the light.

"Love you," they said in unison.

But sleep was slow to come.

~with thanks to artist and intercultural educator Asna Adhami.

Christopher Black

SPEED HOME THE PASSING STRANGER

Speed home the passing stranger,
who comes gently to your door,
whether fleeing hunger,
or cruel, incessant war,
for bound are we by one true law,
that above the rest does reign,
humanity is one shared self and so must share the pain.

Speed home the passing stranger,
whose heart sings of journeys past,
through loss and toil and danger,
and each day feared the last,
for the future is a die yet cast,
and none can know their fate,
but it's easy to extend a hand before it's all too late.

Speed home the passing stranger,
who travels through your land,
seeking refuge from the anger,
to be touched by gentle hand,
for none of us alone can stand,
against the bitter blows of time,
sharing be the only wealth,
all else is but a crime.

Speed home the passing stranger,
who one day may be me,
a solitary wanderer,
long blind, but now can see
that we can have or we can be,
but in the having we must die,
for having is a taking and all the rest's a lie.

Speed home the passing stranger,
who's weary this tired day,
no matter if a sinner
or perhaps has found the way,
for it's what we do instead of say,
that makes us who we are,
we who live together, beneath this saddened star.

Reva Nelson

STREET SHARING

I tried sharing with homeless people when I lived in Toronto, especially the ones in my neighbourhood, who I'd see most often. I never walked by without acknowledging them. At the very least I'd say hello and smile. They had their regular spots outside of my local Shoppers Drug Mart. They'd take turns sharing their piece of cardboard on the sidewalk, as if they had shifts worked out. I gave them money from time to time, not daily but always weekly. One cold, rainy day—that kind of fall day when the chill creeps into your bones—I felt particularly sorry for one of the regulars. He looked colder and more despondent than usual. This time, when I came out of Starbucks with my coffee, I had a latte and a chocolate cupcake for him. He didn't seem appreciative of the $8.49 treat at all.

"You put sugar in that there fancy coffee?" he growled at me. "I'm sure there's sugar on that muffin too. I can't eat that. I'm diabetic. You shoulda asked me first. No one ever asks me first. You fancy people with your fancy coffees. You don't know nothin'."

I apologized and returned with a regular coffee, two milks, no sugar and buttered toast.

"That's better," he said. No thanks as he grabbed the coffee. "Too hot, now I gotta wait."

So much for the sharing beyond the usual toonie, I thought.

About a month later, I was in a different neighbourhood on Eglinton. I went into the bakery to buy a half-dozen bagels and decided to get a dozen for the homeless guy sitting outside. He looked hungry; I thought some food would be better than just change. It took a while for me to get served. I came out with an egg sandwich and the bag of bagels. "My guy" was gone. Not up the street, not down the street, just gone. On my way home I delivered the bagels to my neighbour with three boys, knowing they'd be devoured in minutes. Better them than me. Another thwarted best intention.

I thought giving food would be better than money; a warm drink or something for their bellies might be better than cash for booze or drugs. Did I know that's where their money went? Not for sure, but I could guess. My one regular woman on the corner was on drugs and lived in the neighbourhood crack house. I knew that for sure. Suzy was very skinny, had missing teeth and dull, lank hair. She looked fifty but could have been as young as thirty. Darned if she didn't always speak to me, thank me for my money and tell me to have a good day.

Sometimes we had longer chats; other days she obviously didn't want to talk. I told her I couldn't give her money each day because I lived in the neighbourhood and it would add up, but I would help her out at least weekly. I started to look forward to seeing Suzy, and if she was missing, I worried.

We had lots to talk about. "Nice weather eh?" "Have a good day, Suzy." "Watch the wrestling match last night?" she'd ask. "No, I read a good book though," I'd answer. "See ya got yer hair cut. A bit too short fer ya," she said. "See you didn't." And so on we'd go, with a wee bit of banter, a bit of teasing, just a commentary here and there, on this and that.

One day I was sad, due to a friend's hospitalization and impending death. She told me I looked like hell and asked why. I told her, and then each day she'd ask how my friend was doing. After he died, she told me to wear something red or pink. "That's your best colour. You always look good in red or pink," she declared.

And then, just like that, I had a fashion consultant on the corner. Each day she advised me on what to wear, or not wear. "Why do you have a beige jacket?" she'd ask. "That's not your colour. It does nothing for you. Don't wear beige ever again." The next day, "I like that sweater.

That's good on you." After that, I had my personal wardrobe assistant looking up at me from her cardboard square each and every day. I didn't just get a "Good morning." I got fashion commentary. Suzy felt free to share her expertise with me and I tended to think she was right. One day I gave her a bag of clothes that were too small for me and were everything except pink or red. "Lots of blue and beige in there. Perfect for your colouring," I said. She thanked me and replied, "Ya, I'll look good in these." Sometimes sharing is money, sometimes food, sometimes words. At other times it's fashion advice from an unlikely source.

After I turned fifty, no one noticed me on the street except for "my guys on the corner." There was no more subtle flirting, no sideways glances, no spontaneous smiles. I was invisible. I thought I still looked fine; my friends noticed me, but the casual exchanges from strangers? Gone. So here was Suzy, not just noticing me, but caring enough to share her opinion each day.

I increased her to five dollars per time. Hey, fashion consulting doesn't come cheap.

René Schmidt

STUDENTS STANDING OUT

BETTY-JEAN

"Your mother's on welfare," Betty-Jean whispers to Cody as they stand in line. Cody doesn't react. Neither of them are aware I'm standing right behind them.

Next I hear, "Your clothes come from the Salvation Army, taken off dead people…" Cody flinches. "And your dad is always drunk…"

Cody spins swiftly and hooks a solid rabbit punch to the side of her head; an excellent left hook. Betty-Jean's scarecrow-stiff blond hair splays out like a fan as her head is flung sideways. In the millisecond after his punch Cody sees me and his eyes widen in fear. Betty-Jean remains unaware I'm right behind her. Tough as a twice-cooked steak, she rubs her ear for a moment and returns her hand to her side. Undaunted she croons, "Your mom cooks garbage food from the dumpster…and you eat it."

With a sigh I take them both out of line. Cody rolls his eyes. Betty-Jean's face is creased with innocence.

"Why were you saying those mean things to Cody?"

Her eyes sparkle behind coke-bottle lenses. "What things?"

"How about, 'Your mother gets your food from a dumpster. Your dad is a drunk.'"

"I never said that!"

"I heard you just now, Betty-Jean!"

"I never said a thing. He's making that up."

"Cody hasn't even spoken yet. I am the one who heard you! Me! Standing right here!"

Betty-Jean will never admit to anything. Her family life is as bad as Cody's. Maybe worse. She cultivates her innocent look further. Did she just bat her eyes? I have to turn away to keep a straight face. "And you, Cody, you're not allowed to hit people!"

"What else can I do? I can't beat her at talking."

"You're not supposed to hit. She's a girl."

"Not much of one!"

"I am so!"

"Prove it!"

"You'd like that—pervert face!"

"Stop that!" I hiss.

Kathy the E.A. is watching from the hallway, suppressing a giggle. Usually these scenes don't break out this early. She takes the rest of our Special Education Behavioural class to the library while I deal with the combatants.

"Tell her not to slag my family!"

"Tell him not to be a jerk-off."

"You don't even know what that means!"

"It means you!"

Finally, I send Cody to join the others, his reward for being truthful. My class often has these incidents. After filling a notebook double-sided I stopped writing things down. Today is progress because at least Cody admits he hit her. Betty-Jean is stalwart.

"So why do you do stuff like that?"

"Like what?"

"Insult Cody's family, his clothes, his food. . .all that stuff."

"I never said anything like that."

"For the fifth time, I'm not deaf and I heard you."

"I didn't."

"I said I heard you. So, why?"

She meets my eye and looks away. "Why not?"

"Seriously. Why do you keep bugging him?"

We are in an empty hallway filled with surplus desks. Betty-Jean climbs onto an upside down desk that's piled onto another, one of her favourite places when we have our "little talks." She holds the two upright desk legs like a skier ready to go down a chute, and kicks her legs alternately while I stare, waiting for a reply. This is what we do. I wait and stare and don't let her avoid and she tries to wait me out by avoiding.

Finally, after about ten minutes a single tear slides out of her left eyeball and she quickly wipes it away.

"I fuckin' hate him."

"Why?"

"He's mean to me."

"Why?"

"How do I know why? He just is!"

"You bug him. Why do you do that?"

"He doesn't talk to me. Ever."

"So? Just ignore him."

"Why would I ignore him?"

"Well obviously you don't like him, so ignore him."

"Mr. Schmidt," Betty-Jean looks at me with condescending eleven-year-old wisdom, "I've got the hots for him."

Spectacularly unattractive but confident of her feminine charms, Betty-Jean is fearless as a wolverine and persistent as Attila the Hun. On days she is quiet, does her work and doesn't taunt anybody I call her "my dangerous blonde," and she radiates happiness at the compliment. Her mother is on welfare and her father has long disappeared. She and her mom live hand-to-mouth in a rent-controlled high-rise in Scarborough—one-time luxury buildings with a pool and a sauna and a gym for exercising, but now wastelands of neglect, broken equipment and locked doors.

Lunch time begins finally and a wizened "lunch lady" takes over supervision of my class while Kathy and I go to the staffroom for a much-needed break.

The photographer has left bundles of this year's class photos on the staffroom table for us to distribute and try to collect payment. My pile is the smallest: eight Special-Ed students, Kathy the E.A., and me. Betty-Jean's jarring presence grins from the top of the pile. I wonder if the photographer has put her first as a cruel joke.

Bob, the principal, descends to a new low of professionalism when he holds my class photo bundle up in the staffroom: "Now isn't this a face only a mother could love? I mean, really?" Betty-Jean, grinning through coke-bottle glasses, buck-teeth prominent, and her straight blond hair sticking out like someone touching a Van de Graaff generator. That she had worn a clean blouse that day is not significant. The overall impression is a mixture of all the wrong body parts.

Certainly one of the more unattractive little girls I taught, and likely the most confident. Everything may be stacked against her, but I know she will achieve something in life, *this dangerous blonde.*

SHELBY

Two decades later I am teaching a regular class in a portable at an overcrowded rural school. Being isolated from the regular school noise and interruptions is a welcome change.

Shelby suffers occasional petit-mal seizures. She is the biggest girl in Grade Seven, but so quiet you seldom notice her at the back of the room. The seizures come perhaps once a week, maybe less often. She doesn't flail or struggle but freezes in place and is unable to move or speak. She stares for several minutes, her mouth parted, gulping slightly. Sometimes when the seizure is over she regurgitates a bit of fluid. After it ends, she has no recall of the preceding ten or twenty minutes. While her classmates are understanding of her condition, they keep their distance.

Except Paul. When Shelby is quietly having a seizure, Paul gets up to sit beside her. Ignoring a few titters he places his hand over hers, whispers to her. And as she comes to, he grabs a paper towel and wipes away a small amount of spit that is left on her desk.

His devotion to Shelby is uncomplicated, honest and incredibly touching. It brings a tear to my eye, and I cover up with a manly cough and turn to write on the blackboard. In a community with a high percentage of absentee fathers and divorced parents, and in a school where fights and arguments are constant, this young man reveals adult traits I am proud to witness.

And if they hold hands in class sometimes or sneak a kiss in the schoolyard, I am absolutely and consistently blind to it. The world can only be blessed by couples like this, whatever their age.

From the question: "What do teachers think about student couples?" submitted to Quora in March 2017. 38,000 upvotes and counting.

Alan Bland

THE BAND WAS PLAYING STELLA

The band was playing "Stella by Starlight," one of Victor Young's big movie score numbers from way back. It had been the main theme from *The Uninvited*, a film-noir ghost story from 1944. Ned Washington had written the lyrics to it in 1946, but this band didn't have a singer and had its own take on it. I'd lost track—what do they call it? Oh, right, playing outside. Well I wished that was what they'd do. Take their interpretation outside, maybe down to the garbage dump.

But then I didn't know what that song would come to mean to me. I don't have a problem with what other musicians play—but I don't have to listen to it either. I play alto sax, and I stick with ballads and tunes that my Aunt Jane, if I had an Aunt Jane, could recognize. I had first heard "Stella" on Charlie Parker's version recorded in 1952, and that one had stuck with me.

I was thinking of paying the tab and leaving when the sax and trumpet guys came back around and there we were again, listening to Young's great melody. That was when I looked up and saw the two mugs standing inside the foyer. Maybe it was the fedoras or the polyester plaid sports coats, but they reeked of copper.

Louis, the self-styled maître d' of this humble establishment, conferred with them and then shambled over to my bar stool. It didn't take a Harvard degree to figure these two were on business and were not paying customers.

"I think they are looking for you, Max." That was all he gave me as an introduction before they had me braced against the bar.

"Max Brand? That's you, right?" the older cop, the one in the green fedora asked.

"Yeah, that's me. So what can I do for you gentlemen?"

"You working for Eddy Muldoon?" Brown Fedora asked.

"Yeah, Eddy's a client. And you're not here to play patty cake…so, has something happened to Eddy?"

"You could say that," Green Fedora said. "He's at the morgue. Trouble digesting a bunch of .32s. Is that what you're packing?" His hat was perched up high, resting on two large ears that had taken some beatings over the years.

I flapped open my jacket to show him my piece. "Nah, Colt .38. I'm licenced and it's registered."

"So, where were you earlier this evening?" Brown Fedora asked.

I looked at my watch, surprised to see that it was nearly one o'clock. Maybe the band was better than I'd thought.

"Right here. And you can check that with Louis. And my bar tab."

Detective Sergeant Brown, the green fedora and Detective Green, the brown fedora, took me to the morgue where I had no trouble identifying the late Eddy Muldoon: thief, con-artist, philanderer, forger, but otherwise a really sweet guy.

It was two days later when I next had a visit from someone interested in the late Eddy Muldoon. I was back at the same bar where I'd first learned of Eddy's demise. The band was into its rendition of "Stella by Starlight" again, but this time it was more laid back—the ballad that Victor Young had intended.

This time there were no coppers with their veiled threats and innuendos. This time an apparition stood before me. Petite and blonde with a turned-up nose and sapphire blue eyes. She sported a cute pageboy hair style; her tailored blue shot-silk suit fit her like a glove, the hem of the skirt a modest two inches below her knees.

"Mr. Brand, that is you, isn't it? At least the maître d' said that's who you were," the apparition said.

"Yes, I'm Max Brand, Miss...?" I said, nearly falling off the barstool to take her small hand in mine. Up close I could see that she was a few years older than I'd first thought.

"Stella...Stella Fox. I am...I mean, I was, a...friend, of Eddy Muldoon. The police told me that you were...working for him. I don't know what that means, or what you were doing for Eddy, but I know that he was in some kind of trouble."

"So Miss Fox, what can I do for you?"

"It's Stella. Please call me Stella...Please."

"Okay Stella, so what can I do for you?"

"Well, I would like to see the people who killed Eddy brought to justice."

"And..." I said.

Stella sighed. "Well there is the matter of some Treasury bonds that Eddy was holding for me."

Now I was getting the picture, though still through rose-tinted glasses.

"So, Stella, you want me to find those Treasury bonds?"

Stella perched on a stool and crossed her lovely legs, showing me the first steps on the path to paradise, or maybe perdition. "Well yes, they are rightfully mine, you know."

"And when did you last see them?"

"Oh, well I haven't actually seen them. They belonged to my grandfather and Eddy had tracked them down for me. He told me he had them two days ago but never said where they were. And then he...well...you know what happened."

"So do you think his killer got the bonds?"

"I think that's what I need you to tell me. You're a detective aren't you? A private detective? This is what you do?"

"Yes, that's what I do."

"So can I hire you to find my bonds? And what happened to Eddy, of course. And how much do you charge?"

I had to step back and think. Did I want to take this on to find out who had iced Eddy Muldoon, or simply to stay close to Stella Fox?

"Of course Stella, but I don't see the need to discuss money. I'll do this for Eddy." Stella gave me a look that had my knees knocking. The truth was that Eddy was owed a refund as I hadn't protected him, and he had given me a retainer.

Later Stella and I had somehow ended up at her hotel, where we had drinks, and then dinner and more drinks, then…well then we fell into her bed.

The next morning she showed me what she had to support her claim on the Treasury bonds. It wasn't much. But after last night I didn't need much.

On the surface it looked like Stella had a legitimate claim on the bonds. They had been owned by her grandfather and then passed down to her mother. This was where it became complicated, as her mother had divorced Stella's father and remarried. When that marriage broke apart a few years later Stella's stepfather had ridden off into the sunset with the bonds. Lawyers got involved and an injunction against cashing the bonds froze everybody out until the dispute could be resolved.

At least that was what she told me.

Before the dispute could be resolved the stepfather was killed in a car crash. Nobody was surprised when his car missed a turn and skidded off the road and into fifteen feet of freezing water, as he was a notorious lush. At the inquest the cops said the brakes on his Roadmaster were shot, but that didn't mean that someone hadn't tampered with them. And it didn't explain how the bonds had then surfaced in Eddy Muldoon's possession either.

Later in the evening I drove past Eddy's place, a small clapboard bungalow on the east side of town near the railroad yard. The boards of his crib hadn't seen a lick of paint in a decade and what passed for a garden was covered in junk and knee-high weeds. The landlord already had a "For Rent" sign up, even though the police crime-scene tape was still up around the property.

I figured the tape was still there because nobody had had the time to take it down, so I parked two blocks over and came at the house from the back alley. Cheap-rent houses don't have high-security locks and this one was no different. I waited until the moon was covered by scudding clouds and then I dashed between bushes and onto the back porch. I was inside looking around in less than a minute. My shielded flashlight shone a pencil beam around the kitchen, and the dark stain on the worn linoleum with its chalk outline told me that's where Eddy had died.

I moved through the house. Drawers had been up-ended and cushions thrown on the floor. Bookshelves had been emptied and pictures were askew on the walls, as if the searcher had suspected a hidden safe. Whether the house had been tossed by the police or Eddy's killer was not the issue; it was whether or not they had found the bonds.

I turned off my flashlight, settled into Eddy's faux-leather recliner in the living room and closed my eyes, trying to imagine where Eddy would have hidden the bonds, if he had even had them. I swear I hadn't closed my eyes for more than a minute or two when I heard the front screen door squeak open against its rusty spring, and then a key turned in the lock. The luminous dial on my watch told a different story, that I'd dozed off for nearly an hour. I slipped silently out of the chair and hid behind the curtains.

I could hear a whispered conversation—so there were at least two of them—and the voices seemed familiar. The lights stayed off and I could see the beams from two small flashlights sweeping around the room. I snuck a look from behind the curtain and recognized the profile of Detective Sergeant Brown, his ears protruding like the side mirrors on a transport truck, the green fedora perched above them. Following closely was the brown fedora belonging to Detective Green.

The two detectives moved off through the house and I took the opportunity to sneak back out through the kitchen and into the yard. My illegal entry hadn't gained me much except the knowledge that the cops were interested in the bonds—officially or not. I lurked in the bushes at the side of the house, waiting to see how long Brown and Green were willing to spend searching the house; maybe ripping up carpets and tearing up floorboards. But I had a feeling that Eddy had been smarter than that, and maybe the bonds weren't even in the house.

By two o'clock the two clowns were still inside so I thought that I'd have some fun. I walked down to the local gas station and made a call from the phone on the forecourt, reporting a break-in at Eddy's address. Two minutes later the peace was shattered by wailing sirens, and the street was lit up by flashing lights. Brown and Green tried to make a run to their car but weren't quick enough for the boys in blue.

They were spread-eagled against the side of a cruiser and cuffed before the uniforms would listen to their pleas that they were fellow officers and had a right to be in Eddy's house. It wasn't until the patrolling shift sergeant came by to see what the ruckus was all about that Brown and Green were able to regain their dignity. Although it still took a lot of explaining as to why they were at Eddy's house in the middle of the night.

By three o'clock I figured it was safe to go back in. It took me two hours, but finally I found a large envelope sealed in plastic and taped onto the inside of the cold-air return on the heating system. And inside were the bonds, along with a letter addressed to me.

Max,
If you find this letter and the bonds then I'm gone and you know that I want you to do right by me. I paid you to protect me but what's that worth? If the bad guys want to get you…they will.
If a dame named Stella Fox comes by, well she needs to be taken care of. She is special to me…and not in that way. The bonds are maybe hers, and I won't say they don't have blood

on them. And I won't say how I got them. They've gone through a lot of hands.

A long time ago I was with a gal named Gloria Fox in Phoenix and somehow we had a kid…must be about 30 years old now. I guess I made a lousy father but I want to set some things right. The kid probably got fostered so I need you to track her down and get her set up with a trust, or whatever they call it, so she has a future. But Stella doesn't get given the whole thing until you're sure she's my daughter and that she won't blow it. I'm relying a lot on you Max.

Someone I met in the joint, used to be a lawyer until he got caught diddling the clients' trust funds, said I'd have to give you my Power of Attorney or something. Well this is it, I guess.

You and me Max, we both saved each other's asses in the sandbox, so I know I can trust you. Do it for me, and the kid, Max.

Thanks for being a pal. See you in the big hereafter.

Eddy

My first thought was how to track down Eddy's kid, fostered somewhere around Phoenix, and see if the Stella I'd met really was his daughter. And the second thought was how to deal with Stella, considering that I was now involved with her, which was a definite conflict of interest.

Eddy and I had started out as infantry grunts, not smart enough to know what a spell in the army could lead to; we had been scooped up as smart-assed eighteen-year-olds. We'd teamed up in basic and thought we'd get through our time as a couple of wise guys. Well we hadn't figured out that there were wise guys on the other side too, and that they didn't see the game the same way as us.

Somehow we had both made it home, each sporting a Purple Heart and a gut full of nightmares. When you're hunkered down in a combat zone and just praying to get through the night, you have to trust the guy in the foxhole with you and he has to trust you. And promises made then become promises kept later.

My next thought was who had killed Eddy? And were they now a danger to Stella? And how had Stella and Eddy become entwined in this whole damned affair? Well it looked like Eddy and Stella could be father and daughter, but I'd need a lot more convincing before handing over the bonds.

I used a P.I. contact in Phoenix, an old army buddy who also knew Eddy, to trace any births, deaths, marriages and divorces. It took him a couple of days to fill me in.

Eddy Muldoon had married Gloria Fox after his term in the army. It had been a short-lived marriage ending two years later. In the interim they had been blessed with a daughter whom they had named Stella. So it looked like Eddy and Stella had been telling the truth. I guessed that the bonds had come down from Gloria's side of the family and that Stella had kept her mother's name, Fox. So that left the big questions: Who had bumped off Eddy? And did Stella know that Eddy was her father?

Two days later it started to come together. I couldn't see any reason not to give the bonds to Stella. So I did. Then Brown and Green came by and braced me at the bar just like when I'd first met them.

"Well shamus, this is a good news day," said Brown in the green fedora, with a grin. "We got the shooter who did Eddy Muldoon."

Green in the brown fedora chimed in, "Yeah, just some punk hired to collect on a debt to a bookie. We haven't got the whole thing yet, but it looks like a closed case."

"Kid was a dope-head and when Eddy didn't come up with the cash he owed, the kid just plugged him," said green fedora. "The bookie turned the kid in. Go figure."

So that was it. Maybe the two coppers, Brown and Green, weren't on the make. Maybe they'd just been trying to solve the case. And Stella hadn't been in touch since I'd given her the bonds. I figured she was gone for good and I wouldn't be sharing in her good fortune.

The next night I was sitting on my usual barstool and into my third Scotch and rocks, when the band launched into "Stella by Starlight." And as I looked up the apparition walked into the bar…

Ken and Friends by Dania Madera-Lerman

Kim Aubrey

SPANS

Forty years ago, Miss Tatem taught
me to play Schubert, her pencil marks
still grace these bars, minute numbers

match finger to note, enable hands
to span an octave and more. Miss
Tatem believed in angels, enthused

about their visits during morning
assembly while we girls sat in rows,
smirked, or looked down at our earth

shoes, calculated diminishing angle
of the heel. Miss Tatem believed
I could play Schubert even when I didn't

practice quite enough or skipped
class to play volleyball with boys,
or pleaded shyness to avoid practical

exams only earning certificates
in theory not performance. Easier then
to depend on head, not hands.

Body had already betrayed me, and soon
I'd become a mother whose daughters
would quit piano sooner than I had done,

fed up with their teachers who were far
from angelic, who made me yearn
to go back and work harder.

Ronald Mackay

OUT OF THE MOUTHS OF BABES

During my first few weeks living in the Pensión Méndez in the village of Buenavista del Norte on the Island of Tenerife, my difficulties with Spanish intrigued Doña Lutgarda's grandchildren. Handicaps of any kind tend to erect barriers. Perhaps, however, because little children are closer to the daily struggle of mastering their mother tongue than are adults, the innkeeper's grandchildren were more forgiving of my efforts to make myself understood. Unlike the other adults, I had no work to occupy my days and so they included me as a playmate, albeit larger, older and less linguistically capable than themselves. While they enjoyed their linguistic superiority over that of an eighteen-year-old foreigner, they were unable to fully understand why I was so challenged.

Inevitably, one day I was approached by Caya and her three cousins. They felt the need to get to the source of the novel defect my arrival had brought into their young lives. Caya, aged nine, stepped forward. I could see that she was their spokesman and that the matter was serious.

"Candelita is only three." Her tiny cousin nodded in support of this assertion. "Candelita can speak Spanish. She can even recite in Spanish. Why can't you speak Spanish since you are so much older?"

Caya's nine-year-old logic was impeccable, a request for information to help them understand, rather than an assertion of permanent unfitness. There were entertaining things I could do that they couldn't. Not even their own parents could appear to remove the top half of a forefinger and then restore it to its rightful place, waggle their ears like a helicopter about to take off or make tufts of white cotton wool, one named Peter and the other named Paul, apparently disappear behind my ears and reappear on my fingers at will. Four pairs of eyes and ears awaited my response.

I paused, attempting to cobble together a credible defence. In Spanish, the word for language is *lengua*. *Lengua* also means tongue.

"In Scotland," I began, "in my country we use a different *lengua*—a different *language*."

"You use a different *tongue!*" I had the immediate and undivided attention of five spellbound children, their eyes wide with wonder.

"Yes," I continued. "My first tongue is *inglés*. When I learn it with your help, Spanish will be my second tongue."

There was a pause while they exchanged glances and urged Caya to explain.

"The *Extranjero* already has one tongue and his second tongue will be Spanish!" Caya announced, wide-eyed. She held up two fingers. Gestured to my mouth. Four pairs of eyes examined me intently.

"A second tongue!" The children looked from one to the other, impressed. Full of uncomprehending wonder, they scuttled off to play.

A few short weeks after that incident, I had made great progress with the language. Desperate to be accepted and find a paying job, I'd studied my grammar book and dictionary continuously and practised on every guest in the inn for as long as they had the patience to put up with me. I'd been offered a place on a work gang who were constructing and planting a banana plantation.

One evening I arrived back from work and heard childish laughter coming from the room I occupied in the inn. All five children were going through the many pockets in the tattered, ex-army rucksack that carried the entire sum of my worldly belongings all the way from Scotland through England and France to Cadiz in Spain, where I'd found the boat that brought me to the Canary Islands. They froze the moment I appeared, alarm on their faces.

"*¡Hola!*" I greeted cheerfully. Their eyes were downcast in guilty silence. "What are you doing?"

"Nothing!"

"Are you looking for something?" I tried to sound reassuring.

Judging from the children's uneasy silence I was not going to get an answer to this question, so I lifted my old rucksack off the floor onto the bed.

"What would you like to see?" I possessed nothing of value except my passport and a camera I had bought in Gibraltar but seldom used because the cost of film was exorbitant. Even what I intended to be a reassuring question brought a tiny quiver to Candelita's lower lip. I had to be careful to avoid causing tears.

"I'm not angry," I tried to reassure them, "I'm simply curious." Relief flooded their faces. Candelita's lip stilled. "I've already shown you everything I have, but if you like, I'll show it all to you again." I offered a smile.

The children stood in a silent line, eyeing their nine-year-old leader, willing her to speak for them. Caya appreciated her leadership role and her young face took on an almost-adult seriousness.

"Do you remember," she began, and as she spoke her confidence returned. "Do you remember that day when you told us that you were going to get Spanish to be your second tongue?" My nod encouraged her. "Well, my Grandmother told us that you now possess that second tongue. That's why you were able to find a job in the banana plantation." She paused. I was trying to follow her gist. I smiled encouragement. "Well, now that you have your second tongue, we are searching for your first one."

Four little heads nodded in sober agreement, eyes bright with contrition but more confident now that they'd been assured my forgiveness.

"We promise to handle it carefully!" Fonfon's eyes were enormously large.

"We just want to see what your first tongue looks like." Candelita's face glowed. "We want to see the difference between them." Her eyes widened in anticipation.

Caya was more pragmatic. "You won't tell Mamá, we opened your rucksack, will you?"

Their idea of what it takes to be bilingual left me in awe. Substitute tongues that can be slipped into place with a simple *click!* to meet the linguistic demands of the moment. Would that it were so easy! But how to reveal to young minds that the solution doesn't lie with replaceable anatomy? I was lost for words to explain how the single Spanish word *lengua* serves two completely different purposes. One refers to the system of sounds and words we use to communicate with family and friends; the other to the pliable muscle we mould, point, curve and flex to create the sounds that express what we feel and allow others to understand us.

"Of course, I'm not going to tell your Mamá!" It was all I could think to say. It was all they wanted to hear. Off they trooped, with grateful looks, but without the understanding I would like to have shared with them. Their years were too tender to be burdened with stark facts about how difficult most of life's many challenges would turn out to be.

Esther Sokolov Fine

LITTLE SHOCKS

My grandmother almost always had a piece of thread dangling from her lower lip. She hummed Yiddish melodies and used a push-pedal sewing machine that needed repair. Eventually it was retrofitted into a portable case that could be carried back and forth between our modest home on Lilac Street and Auntie Rosie's more lavish establishment. The remodelled Singer had a safety socket and an electric foot pedal, but I wasn't allowed near it. A wayward needle could go straight to your heart and cause you to die within a very short time. My mother didn't want to take the risk.

I, second shortest member of the third-grade choir, was to be dressed as an elf, red down one side and green down the other, with stiff lining and bells on the tips of pointy-toed boots. Gramma Tillie sewed my costume. I watched as she bit off the tail end of thread for the Christmas pageant boots. At showtime I was moved to the back row of the choir because my toes were wrong; they curled up too high and then flopped over, but like the words of the songs, it wouldn't matter as long as I moved my lips and hit the right notes. No one could see me back there anyway.

The daddies used to shuttle Gramma Tillie back and forth in their cars. My father delivered her to Collingwood Avenue on Thursday evenings in our rusty 1941 Chevy. Uncle Sammy returned her on Sunday nights in his shiny black Lincoln Continental with windows that glided up and down with the touch of a magic button. Toward the end of 1949, when new models were rolling off the Detroit assembly lines, our Chevy died on Beldon Avenue (exactly halfway between

Collingwood and Lilac), and we had to call a cab. I was glad. I imagined that we too might get automatic car windows.

Gramma Tillie sang, sewed, cooked, baked enormous poppy seed coffee cakes, and washed dishes in both houses. She had to be on Collingwood with Rose and Sam on Friday mornings so that she could go to her Reading Club at the Workmen's Circle. She had to stay there until Sunday night so that my father could rule the Lilac Street domain on his two days off.

Uncle Sammy, a frustrated opera singer with a beautiful tenor voice, loved to sing standing next to the piano, while Auntie Rosie accompanied, with a living room full of guests chiming in. "Some Enchanted Evening" was a favourite. Sammy sang everywhere: in the house, on the street, even waiting in line for movies. This did not appear to embarrass his family.

If it had been *my* father singing we would have pretended not to know him, and my mother would have whispered, "Oh, Eugene, please not here," but that never happened. She had carefully married silence. While he enjoyed music, he couldn't carry a tune and barely spoke. Perhaps he couldn't see the use of conversation, or maybe he had so much to say he didn't know how to begin. He voiced his thoughts in undercurrents, asides, whispered puns, and sarcastic jokes that only the attentive would hear and only the clever could understand.

"If your Chevy could only have one gear, which one would you choose?" Cousin Oscar asked my father one day.

"Reverse," he answered.

The scene is Sunday evening, early 1949. We are visiting Auntie Rosie and Uncle Sammy in their house on Collingwood Avenue. I am in the downstairs bathroom, shivering because the outer hallway where the bathroom is located is unheated. While it has both hot and cold running water and a black and white ceramic tile floor, like an outhouse this bathroom has a brown wooden toilet seat, which is ice cold to the touch in wintertime. I'm eight. I have been in this bathroom for a while.

I have already flushed and am listening to the toilet's incessant cry. Its song is like a badly tuned violin starting at high A flat and whining down a minor scale toward the basement. The ghostly sound emanates from aged pipes as the tank slowly refills itself for the next guest.

I have washed my hands with strong smelling brown Fels Naphtha soap, when I am surprised to discover that there is no towel in the usual place and no reserve supply of toilet paper. I'm trying to figure out how, with wet hands, I might safely turn off the light. To do so would require me to pull on the long string that hangs from a ceiling fixture. I panic. My mother has for years cautioned me in preparation for this moment, and I sense that I have very few choices. I can decide to dry my hands on my clothing and thereby mess up my skirt. This will disturb my mother, who has carefully dressed me for this evening. I can leave the light on, a forbidden act in this house, which will bring Uncle Sammy's wrath upon me. I can call for help, which could bring forth a torrent of teasing from the cousins. Finally, I can risk electrocution.

My mother's teachings grew partly out of her fear that I might someday succumb to my father's science lessons and become attracted to electricity, or simply stand by, intrigued, as my younger brother Joe poked a pencil or a fork into an electrical socket. From her own childhood, she often dredged up a story, telling it vividly as if it were a recent catastrophe. She had been a young child, visiting relatives in Atlantic City with her parents and her sister. Their host family had a little girl just like me. In the voice of omniscient narrator, she told me that during their visit the girl had stood on the bathroom sink, and with wet hands she had reached up and touched a burning light bulb to see if it was hot. She was instantly electrocuted. Killed. Dead at seven years old. A cautionary tale and only partly true, but it shocked me in just the way my mother intended. Another family story was that, as a child, my father liked to go down to the basement, poke his finger into the fuse box, and give himself mild shocks. The threat of sudden death loomed over my childhood.

"Never go without breakfast," my mother warned.

"Tillie Lapidus's granddaughter was in the hospital with a shrunken stomach for months because she stopped eating for a whole summer at camp, just because she wanted to lose weight," added my grandmother.

Having survived his childhood, my father grew up to be an electrical engineer. Though he never practised this professionally, he solved electrical problems. He'd get calls from relatives on Saturday mornings and go rushing off to save the day for uncles, aunts, cousins, and even neighbours. The reason, we were told, that he never practised engineering professionally, was that he graduated during the later years of the Depression, just before World War II, when there were few positions in the field. He didn't go to war because his job with the City of Detroit Civil Service Commission was considered a "critical occupation." Instead he served in our neighbourhood, keeping watch as an air raid warden.

My father liked to jaywalk and spit out of the car window. His aim wasn't great. I learned that it was unsafe to keep the back window of the car rolled down. He wanted me to score well on IQ tests. He wanted me to speak flawless English, even though he often spoke as if he had grown up in a back alleyway. He spoke that way on purpose, when he wanted to sound tough, but he had a sophisticated grasp of English and expected perfect speech from his two children. He would have been happier if I had placed better than seventh in the school spelling bee. "Deny," that was the word that got me.

My mother too had survived a shock. Her childhood diary stopped abruptly just before her sixteenth birthday at the time of her father's suicide. My mother wanted to insulate *me* against shock. I was to lead a cautious life, be virtuous, tactful, and always kind to children who had less. I was to be honest and clean, a good sister, to say yes if a boy asked me to dance (especially if he was Jewish), and cross at the corner.

So, when I, the eight-year-old product of this electrifying history, stand frozen in the downstairs bathroom on Collingwood Avenue, trying to identify the least of four evils, I choose. With hands still wet, I reach up, grab the long string, shut my eyes tight, clench my teeth, and pull. I hear a click. Everything goes dark and still. I feel my heart pound as I stand waiting for the shock of my death.

Teeth chattering, I catch a whiff of fresh coffee percolating in the kitchen. I hear soft rumbles of laughter and "Some Enchanted Evening" calling me to the living room. Still trapped in the cold dark bathroom and still breathing, I try to grab the doorknob, but my hands are slippery. The toilet has stopped singing. Desperate and shivering, I put my hand just under the hem of my dress, and wrapping the soft fabric around my fingers and then around the doorknob, I turn it. I push open the door to the entrance hall and run to my mother who is having a cigarette break in a far corner of the living room.

"I did a terrible thing," I cry to her.

"What?"

"I touched the string with wet hands to turn off the light."

"You what?" shriek the cousins, bursting into laughter.

Uncle Sammy stops singing and turns his harshest gaze on my mother. Their eyes lock. "What kind of nonsense are you teaching her? You've scared her half to death."

Now it is my mother who stands frozen. Her eyes move to the door, then her feet to the hall closet. Winter coats, boots, hats, gloves, my father, my brother Joe, all of these have to be found and gathered up quickly. She wants to be out before dessert is served.

Drying her hands on her "aprom" (she always pronounced it aprom), Grandma Tillie whispers loudly to me from the kitchen doorway and blows a kiss. "Goodnight, Momala. Be good to your mother, she gets nervous."

The Chevy is parked in the driveway. We watch our breath escape into the cold air as we settle into the car. My mother curls up in the backseat with little Joe, who is nearly asleep. I sit up front.

"I'm sorry, Mummy, I didn't want to make Uncle Sammy mad," I whisper as we speed out of the driveway in reverse to begin our long trip back to Lilac Street, where my mother can be the best musician on the block and make up her own rules as she goes along, designing her own enchanted evenings.

Marie Arden Prins

A SHARED NAME, AN UNSHARED LIFE

My grandmother shares my name. And I share hers. It is a name of love and loss, given to me before my birth. The name of a woman whose flesh and blood formed the woman who formed me. The name of a grandmother pictured in a 5-by-7 black-and-white photograph that rests on my mother's living room end table. In it she stands next to my grandfather in their backyard, her head slightly tilted, a soft yet no-nonsense expression on her face.

Gram and Pop Wisse c. 1945

For most of my life, this photo was merely a vague testament to a woman I never missed because her memory was seldom invoked. Her early death had generated a gap in my family's history. But recently, I've gleaned photographs from a crumbling album and gently mined my mother's fading memories to reclaim my *grootmoeder* who died before I was born. She rose out of the shadows of another century, another country, and another culture, all left behind when she married my grandfather and crossed the ocean to begin a new life with him in northern New Jersey.

Marie Buijze was born in 1889 in the Netherlands, in the southern province of Zeeland, which is a cluster of large islands reclaimed from the sea and anchored to the continent by Belgium. Not far from this border lies the small city of Terneuzen with its surrounding towns where my ancestors lived for centuries, some in the countryside, some by the sea, and a few in the city itself.

My grandmother was the eldest of nine children, three of whom died in infancy. She was born and raised in a two-room *workmans* house covered in grey stucco and roofed in red clay tiles, a house built on *de Baandijk* that stretched out of Terneuzen along a ditch and into the countryside.

My grandmother's father, Adriaan, was a farm labourer. He toiled from dawn to dusk for a wealthy farmer and little money, which led towards his early death. During the growing season, Adriaan also tilled a half-acre of land on the *polder* behind his house to feed his expanding family. It yielded most of their food for the year.

My grandmother's mother Rachel was a Dutch housewife who kept their house spotless. She prepared the family's meals on a cook stove in the small kitchen that contained a dry sink, a cupboard, and a sturdy table with chairs. A wooden ladder led to the *zolder* where the older children slept under the eaves.

In the front room, or *beste kammer*, white curtains framed two windows. Between them sat an heirloom table and hutch that held the

Sunday china. Wasting no space, the middle wall enclosed two beds behind panelled doors—one for Marie's parents and the other for younger children.

While the front door was opened only on formal occasions, the back door was the portal to the outer world. One step down was a small stoop and an iron pump fixed above a cistern. To the left was the WC, harbouring spiders. To the right, around a corner, was the pigpen and an enormous pig. A small shed housed farm implements and chickens, which Rachel raised for eggs.

After she was born, Marie was swaddled in layers of clothing to protect her from the *waterkould*, the chilly dampness of Holland that seeps into the bones. As a young girl she wore thick undergarments and a heavy skirt and blouse over which she wrapped a striped apron. She pulled woolen stockings up her legs and squeezed her feet into *klompen*, wooden shoes. In warmer weather she often went barefoot. Later, as a young woman, Marie's clothes resembled her mother's outfits of warm shirts, bulky vests with *flaaren* (wings) and woolen skirts. She wore a white cap on her head with a braid hanging down her back. In time she acquired a strand of orange coral beads, or *koraalen*, for church or special occasions.

Marie Buijze's early life was little different from that of generations of girls and women who lived before her. The Dutch family was virtuous, frugal, and hard-working. The father was the provider, the mother the housewife, and the children subordinate to their parents. In the southern part of Zeeland where the Buijzes lived, the Dutch Reformed Church was the pillar of society. Respect for its authority and adherence to its beliefs were paramount in daily life.

Dutch law required all children to attend school until they turned twelve. It is likely that my grandmother learned to read and write in a school with two rooms, one for boys and the other for girls. Along with math and geography, she was taught sewing, darning, and knitting skills.

After Grade Four or Five, she returned home to help her mother with the endless household chores and the care of her younger siblings.

Life on *de Baandijk* was not all hard work. Sundays provided a break from the grind of daily life. Dressing in their Sunday best and walking to church dominated the larger part of the day. But afterwards, there was visiting with friends and family, drinking coffee in the *beste kammer,* eating a hearty meal, and probably attending another church service in the early evening. A favourite pastime was debating Sunday sermons and interpretations of scripture. They dove into it with a passion that often stretched into the rest of the week and sometimes into family and church schisms.

As Marie grew into adulthood, she became restless living in the small *workmans* cottage. Family lore reveals that my grandmother had an independent streak. As soon as her sisters could take over household chores, Marie spread her wings and left home in 1909. She donned Western dress and went to work for a merchant family in Terneuzen as a nursemaid for their little girls. She also minded their *winkel,* or small dry goods store, when the children attended school or when the parents ate their midday dinner.

Wages were low for domestics and Marie may have earned no more than 50 to 100 guilders a year. Some if not all of this money may have been turned over to her family. But some may have been squirrelled away for her future. No longer a country girl, Marie had taken a decisive step into adulthood and the world of city life. Her expanded horizons grew, and five years later, gave her the courage, determination, and finances to leave her provincial Dutch life when she married my grandfather, Jan Adriaan Wisse.

Born in 1887, my grandfather was the second eldest child of another large family. His father Wilhelm was a *visser* or fisherman, his mother Adrianna a traditional Dutch housewife who bore sixteen children, five of whom died as infants. As an older boy, Jan also worked on a *botter* in the Westerschelde River that separated Zeeland from the rest of Holland. He dubbed for flounder, sorted fish, and coiled ropes. The work was always hard and often dangerous. Boats, wharfs, fish, ropes, nets, baskets—all were wet, cold, and slippery, especially in stormy and wintery weather. So as a young man, my grandfather decided to learn masonry.

When my grandparents began to court, Jan was 22, Marie 20. He was a city boy, she a country girl. But they may have gone to school together or attended the same church every Sunday. Or maybe Jan brought fresh fish to the *winkel* or patched the bricks on the merchant's building. How they met is unknown, but given their small social world, they more than likely knew each other for a long time before Marie's independent streak caught Jan's eye and Jan's hard-working spirit convinced Marie that he was a good catch.

In the spring of 1911, the Wisse family made the momentous decision to leave the Netherlands. The year before, Wilhelm had declared bankruptcy as he could no longer earn enough to feed his large family and pay their debts. Five years earlier, his older brother's family had emigrated to the United States. They had settled in northern New Jersey and found work in its textile mills. Undoubtedly, they wrote home about the economic prospects available in this Land of Opportunity.

At this time it was common for whole families to emigrate together. The young, unmarried adults and older teenagers found employment and helped establish their families in the new country. So Jan's family sold most of their possessions to pay the steep $45-per-person price for eleven tickets on the *SS Ryndam* of the Holland America Line. On April 8 the Wisse family left Rotterdam for America. Ten days later they arrived in Hoboken, New Jersey. The ship manifest states they had $90 in their pockets and planned to live with Oom Anthony Wisse in Passaic. My grandfather Jan was described as a 23-year-old merchant, 5 feet 6 inches, with black hair and blue eyes. He was actually a mason and carried a certificate documenting his trade, a profession he pursued for years.

When Jan immigrated to America, my grandparents had not announced an engagement. But two and a half years later, Jan returned to Zeeland with a notarized document from his parents (necessary for "children" under 30) that granted him permission to marry. On December 24 1913, Jan and Marie announced their engagement and were married three weeks later on January 15 in the Terneuzen Townhall. Afterwards their families and friends gathered for a wedding ceremony in Nordstraat Christian Reformed Church. Before their simple reception of traditional Dutch foods, Marie and Jan posed for a formal wedding portrait. Jan had become John and sported a western suit, while Marie wore a black skirt and blouse with a brocade vest. In her hands she held the black gauze veil she'd worn during the ceremonies. Around her neck hung a long gold chain, a wedding gift from her in-laws. She did not wear her *koraalen* necklace. Nor did she wear a Dutch cap or hat of any kind. She too preferred the ornaments and dress of her future.

John and Marie Wisse, Wedding 1914

Honeymoons for Holland's working poor were an extravagance the newlyweds could not afford. Instead, after all the paperwork had been filed at the town hall and Marie's emigration papers received, the couple travelled to Rotterdam, passed through a thorough inspection, and finally boarded the *SS Noordam* on February 14, 1914. John had purchased second class tickets. For twelve days they savoured the luxury of a small, private cabin with running water, hours of relaxation in the lounges, bracing walks on the deck, and hotel-quality meals three times a day with entertainment in the evenings, all a foretaste of the prosperity available to them in the United States. When they disembarked at the Holland America Line port in Hoboken, New Jersey, John's family greeted them, hoisted their baggage onto their shoulders, and motored them to the Wisse home on Gregory Street in Passaic, New Jersey.

Within two years, despite World War I having broken out in Europe, Marie and John had moved into their own clapboard house on "Dutch Hill." John had obtained steady work as a mason and Marie had a newborn baby to raise. In their first American studio portrait, John stiffly held his son on his lap, while Marie, wearing a white muslin dress and her gold chain, stood next to him, a small smile playing on her lips. Her eyes were underlined with the dark circles of motherhood, but her gaze was proud and direct. Their small family was already reaping the rewards of their momentous decision to move thousands of miles to the prosperity of the New World.

However, while Marie and John's house was more spacious, their material possessions more plentiful, and their food more varied, their lives replicated in profound ways the one left behind in Zeeland. Like their ancestors, the Wisses were a frugal, virtuous, hard-working, traditional family. John was the head of the household and Marie a mother and housewife, though often an equal partner in financial and family decisions. Their children, much loved, toed the line. But above all, the Dutch Christian Reformed Church and its beliefs and customs remained the centre of their world. Regular Sunday church attendance (three services, one in Dutch), private Christian school for their children, weekly church committee meetings, and a social life comprising extended family and church members defined their lives. For Marie and John much had changed, but much remained the same.

To tie Marie's new American life to the old Dutch one of her close-knit family in Zeeland, many letters penned in Dutch crossed the ocean. Only once did she travel back to visit them in Holland. In 1936, two years after Marie's father Adriaan had died, John purchased tickets on a cargo ship *The Black Tern* for Marie, himself, and my nine-year-old mother. Now and then, stories of that trip, and a few others of my mother's childhood were shared with me and my siblings. But not many. And not often. Life was busy in my house. My parents had five children to raise and full-time jobs. There seemed little time to tell tales of past lives, especially those of my grandmother whose life ended too soon. Memories of my much-loved grandmother were held tightly within my mother's heart. Now, as I poke and prod, she shares memories of both parents and a childhood lived in that Dutch immigrant enclave of Northern Jersey. From a few photographs and much research, plus emails from my Dutch cousin Adrie, I have imagined my grandmother's early life in Zeeland. Seven decades after she died, I am finally meeting my grandmother, even though I never sat on her lap and brushed her long hair or baked Dutch sweets in her kitchen or listened to stories of the old country. Mercifully, we share a name that finally sparked a desire, almost too late, to find her and fill that gap in my life.

"A Shared Name, an Unshared Life" is excerpted from a larger memoir piece to be shared with family, friends, and the wider North American Dutch community when completed.

Michael Topa

COMMUNITY

I imagine the first primitive cells in porous caves
      of iron sulfide near a
warm ocean vent struggling to build their tiny
      houses in great darkness

All of us reside too in separate habitats in helter-
      skelter of private thought
while silence billows like random clouds we are
      oscillating spheres adrift

in an endless universe without walls When we go
      outside from the heart's
shuttered shop let us then thatch together a new
      shelter against isolation

knowing that Eros is the primordial fountain in
      which we are free to undress
and bathe that community is where we find our
      unborn self in each other

Felicity Sidnell Reid

ELEGY FOR ANCIENT BONES

Bug River spreads
in summer heat
streams of cool
water through
a glass lake.
Trout inhale swinging
currents sinking
into mud.
The water level falls.
Winter skinned
the river bank, tearing
soil from ancient
bones.
And now they lie
exposed.
A fisherman
could hardly know
how long those bones
had lain below
the soil.
And yet…in spite of…
yes—despite a faint
suspicion of their
ancient provenance
he reported the find.
And so we know a

man was buried there
beneath a capping stone
5000 years ago.
Knowledge shared—
new safer resting place?

Margaret Kropf

LULLABY TO THE SKELETON

Sleep, sleep, Mr. Boneclacker,
Hang still in sleep,
In the mist of the night
When the shadows are deep,
And the long, dreary wind
Sticks a thumb in the pane,
And the icy twigs snap
In the skittering rain.

Now a jangle of bolts
In a long, empty cell
That once housed a mind,
Yet those bones suit you well.

Never fear, Mr. Boneclacker,
Luckier you,
Though you're riven with holes
That the shows seep through
And you're propped up with pegs,
For you've freedom to dream,
And not one pretension.
You are what you seem.
In your passionless pose
And your sexless attire
You've something in you
That our flesh can admire.

Sleep, sleep Mr. Boneclacker,
Brittle and bare,
With hard, bony scowl
And pitiless stare.
Sleep, sleep when the wind
Sticks a thumb in the pane
And the icy twigs snap
In the skittering rain.

Diane Taylor

THAT SINKING FEELING

It's Monday. I pull on my navy pea jacket, wrap a turquoise scarf around my neck, don gloves and step out into the cool crispness of the late November morning. That first feel of the outdoors rushing into my nostrils astonishes me, and I feel how wonderful it is to be fully alive, fresh oxygen reaching all parts of my body. I smile at the air and breathe deeply. I look about me to see what I can see, hear what I can hear.

Pausing in my driveway, I watch a black squirrel gather a mouthful of dead leaves from the crook of a maple tree. It carries them up high where it relays them to another squirrel, which then carries them to a large collection of leaves that is a nest. I have never seen squirrels co-operate in homebuilding before and am struck at how close to the rhythms of the seasons I am in this small urban centre. I feel instantly linked to the natural processes of the earth.

I stride out onto the sidewalk for my walk to town. Passing my property, I look over the gardens on the front lawn. All is orderly, though I'll have to rake leaves soon—do my own collection of the last of the trees' formidable fallen foliage.

Something catches my eye. What is that? Looks like a hole at the far edge of my property. I walk over. What? It *is* a hole!

Who did this? That is my first thought, and a loud one it is.

My next thought is to examine the hole closely and calmly. Now, I'm a fairly calm person. I meditate regularly. I know from Buddhist readings that we are better off if we don't submit to fear because that just generates mental gossip. However, I can feel the adrenaline rushing into my brain, heart, eardrums, spine. Gone is the exhilaration of fresh November air.

Like a scientist, I squat to get a closer look and do a hand measurement. I know my hand span is nine inches, and the hole measures a very even eight inches by twenty. It is a foot and a half deep, and earth has been scooped out under the grass for another foot. Very strange. There is no earth scattered on the surface, so it cannot have been a squirrel, skunk, cat or dog. Because the hole is so precise in rectangular shape, it has to have been excavated by a machine. But for what purpose?

My first suspect is my next-door neighbour, because we share a property line and occasionally have boundary discussions, and because I keep pushing him to repair his fence that blew down three years ago. Does this have something to do with a new fence? But why is it on my side only? Is he trying to establish a new boundary and gain inches? I know where Eddy works, so I continue on my walk and drop in on him at his auto body shop. Did he know anything about a hole? I watch him carefully to detect any attempt at pulling a fast one on me, but his round pink face is clear of subterfuge as he blinks, says no, he has no idea.

My next suspect is the town. I knew that my street was slated for widening at some point in the future, and I was concerned that widening would take away some of my already skimpy front yard. I had recently written the town a letter voicing my concerns, saying I was worried my property would decrease in value if it was any closer to the road. I suggested the sidewalk should stay on "my" side so as to keep a buffer between me and the road, and that the town consider a crosswalk further up the street. Is the town trying to establish a marker for the location of the new road? The hole is a good six feet beyond where I know the town line to be, so this worries me. But can they just come and dig a hole to mark a worksite without consulting me? I can feel myself heating up to do battle—completely forgetting that I am a wannabe Buddhist who observes her mind and controls her thoughts.

At the town hall, a few blocks past the auto body shop, I remind myself to be reasonable, polite. Perhaps there is a rational answer.

Perhaps we can work it out. The woman at the desk says she knows of no work being done on my street and suggests I walk over to Public Works just around the corner. There, a woman phones the man who is in charge of roadwork and he says, no, nothing is happening on my street. She suggests I call Bell and Veridian, but I know where the phone and hydro lines are and the hole is nowhere near them.

No cause for alarm, I tell myself. But I will defend my land if I have to!

I walk home prepared to do more research. *Who* is responsible for the hole?

I have barely taken off my jacket when there's a knock at the door. It's Samuel from the Roads Department. He says he has worked for the town for thirty years and thought he'd better have a look. His gaunt face is brown and weathered and he doesn't crack a smile. Neither do I. We are in investigative mode.

"Let's see this hole," he says in what I perceive as a know-it-all kind of way, which makes me immediately skeptical of his forthcoming opinion.

I slip on my jacket and we walk out to the hole.

He doesn't study it. He knows what it is.

"It's a sinkhole," he says.

A sinkhole? No. Sinkholes happen in Miami, Los Angeles, all over Toronto. Not in my town. Not in my yard. This is not believable. But that's not what I say.

"A sinkhole?"

"Yep."

"You're sure?"

"Looks like it. Could be an old well or drainage tile, or all the rain we've had. I've seen them before in Port Hope."

"Where have you seen them?"

"There's one right now in front of the Idea Hub building on Peter Street. A small car would fit into it. We don't know what caused that one either."

"My goodness…" I observe my mind do a 180-degree shift. This man knows his town.

I can see what I've done: something I think I don't do. I have jumped to a conclusion without allowing for the possibility that there could be an answer I hadn't thought of. I have stereotyped the situation with limited knowledge. I blamed someone—anyone—in the blink of an eye. That was my first response to perceived danger.

My question should have been *how*, not *who*.

Why didn't I remember Malcolm Gladwell's book, *Blink?* He shows how the rush of adrenaline and a racing pulse interfere with good judgment. I see how it can happens that people are wrongfully convicted. I just did it myself.

Who'd have thought that there could be a hole in my front yard that was not man made? That's the thing…I didn't think. But even had I taken the time to give the phenomenon some thought, was there anything in my background that would have leapt into view? Maybe, just maybe, if I had emptied my mind of its incriminating fist, there would have been space for me to receive the memory of an old well at the house I lived in during my high school years in the fifties. My parents liked the look of the days-of-old pump that stood off to one side of the back door. However, when Dad extended the driveway to include that space, the picturesque pump had to go and the well had to be filled with gravel. A few months later, a depression appeared where the well had been, and it had to be filled again. How much time or reflective intelligence would it have taken to search back to the past?

So, my lesson is double edged. First, I have what it takes to stereotype. Oh, that's a hard one. Second, I am not in danger! At least not today. But what if another sinkhole appears? What if it is 300 feet wide as some are? What if it is under my house? What if…?

I sigh, and smile at my foolish, perhaps somewhat wiser, self. Well, time will tell.

Tuesday dawns red as a promise. Eddy waves to me at my kitchen window as he leaves for work, and I wave back. The town comes to fill in the hole. The squirrels settle into their cozy winter quarters. Equanimity restored, I slip into my jacket and step out into the cool friendliness of this November morning.

Wally Keeler

FALL OF THE EMPLOYED

There has been a massive layoff of leaves throughout the northern hemisphere of Earth. Leaves demanded higher rates of sunlight, lighter showers and heavier dew. The oxygen production industry declined the demands. Chlorophyll withdrew its succulents. Sap plummeted. Streets throughout the deciduous world clogged themselves with unemployed leaves.

Depleted avenues have had their abundant diversity blown away by the forwarded forces of the One-Colour Regime. Whiteness is coming. Chill goosebumps the land. Timber shivers in a shakedown of residuals of warmth.

The local media continue to ignore this event. In front of the offices of Northumberland Muse, the unemployed litter the sidewalk but not a word about their plight can be found in its austere pages.

Unsettling reports of abuse and cruelty towards the unemployed leaves have been pouring into the environmental protection agencies. Residents are rounding up the unemployed, bagging them for final disposal.

Some unemployed leaves have fallen on hard times and lie in the gutters of community where children and childish adults kick them about in the chuffle[1]

---

[1] Coined by Wally Keeler, 2001, embedded in an article about poetry as Child's Play Is Wild Play, describing how children chatter and shuffle—chuffle.

"Yesterday I saw children coming out of the church and cross the street to kick about the sullen unemployed with unbridled glee," said Rainbow Stardust. "It's just tree trash anyway!"

"I saw a swarm of children in Victoria Park yesterday, wallowing in laughter and unemployed leaves with such intensity that leaves scurried away with cold-shoulder breezes," said Toby McClintick.

Jessica Outram

SMUDGING FEATHER

My cousin and I started smudging together in the 1990s. Aunt Pat gave us our first sage and abalone shell bowls. We learned about ceremony. We learned about the value of sharing sacred time together.

Last summer I bought a beautiful smudging feather with a pink quartz handle that stands proudly in an oak base. It was created by First Nations artist LinDaLou. The staff at The Whetung Ojibwa Centre told us that the artist visits the Centre, setting up a table by the fire for a few days to assemble them. We loved that it was created in a space that means so much to us.

When my cousin visits, we usually go to the Centre in Curve Lake First Nation. For twenty years we've travelled there to become inspired, to connect to the past, to learn more about our story, to collect pieces that call to us.

I'm not sure why I picked up the feather. I guess it was just a way of interacting with the wonderful things on display. I do that when I'm shopping: pick up things and hold them. When I held the feather for the first time I knew it had chosen me. Its energy moved through my hand and radiated leadership, voice, identity, and destiny. The room seemed brighter. Holding the feather, I became the best version of myself, overcome with strength and clarity and gratitude.

I would later describe it as a Harry Potter moment, like when Harry's wand selected him at Ollivanders in Diagon Alley. It did not feel like an ordinary moment or an ordinary feather. I did not want to put the feather back on the shelf. I carried it around the store for an hour while I looked at other things. My goal was to buy a new key chain and some books on this trip. Well, I ended up buying a feather too.

We got home from the gallery around 6:00 p.m. The feather was in my living room only twenty minutes before I began pulling books off shelves.

"This is not going to work," I said. "These books don't want to be here anymore."

"Yes!" my cousin replied. "Do it now. I love it."

And so we rearranged books, furniture, and all my treasures for hours on a Sunday evening, transforming the house, restoring balance, inspired by and sharing the feather's energy.

Then it was time to light the sage and begin the smudging. We were so thrilled to use the feather that we forgot to open the windows. My house filled with a thick smoky sage haze, but we didn't mind because we were happy and at peace (and so was the house).

Nearly a year later, the feather continues to inspire me to find balance, to use my voice, and to trust my intuition.

My cousin shared with me the importance of honouring our Anishinaabe roots as Métis people. We can learn so much from family.

Miigwetch, Whetung Ojibwa Centre.

Maureen Mullally

CRYSTAL HEARTS

Another crystal heart showed up today. I brushed the dirt off it and placed it on a window ledge.

A message?

I persuaded myself it was.

The late summer day was cool, inviting me to plant a new clematis. There were attractive sales at the gardening centres. It was time I replaced some perennials, and the flowering climber, I had promised myself. I'd take a trip to town and see what the gardening centres had.

"This one is wonderful, easy to grow, never stops blooming, look at all the buds still to come out, you'll love it."

Well, I think Paulina said that, in between her ceaseless stories of her two sons, middle-aged men working in Toronto and receiving big bonuses at work, coming home to help when they could. I remembered these boys chasing each other with the nursery's water hose many years ago. Then she asked if I had heard of the robbery she'd had—that it cleaned out some greenhouses, messed up two more, broke stuff. Help was hard to get, and mother died at 92 still working in the nursery, coming here from Europe every year...

I have known Paulina and her family for many years; her nursery stock is the best, but you do have to be prepared for the lady herself. She is amazing, and exhausting. I was too confused to question her further and finally paid for my treasures and made my getaway.

Home again, I made myself a coffee, sat on my sunny deck and pondered my new arrivals. I then got myself in gear to plant my lovely new plants. I had the ideal location, a wall in the sun with a trellis already installed. Unfortunately the soil was poor and rock hard; I would need to do some digging and replace it.

I dug the bed, removed some of the hard earth and prepared the hole for the vine. I needed some good soil to build up the bed again. Luckily I had some magic ingredients.

My bagged soil mixed well with the beautiful black compost that fell readily from the bottom door of my compost container.

Many years ago when we were still living in England, my late husband Brian worked for a master gardener and learned the magic of composting. Ever since those days we have always had a composter of some kind. I now have two large plastic bins with air vents on the sides. I still marvel at the whole process: All my veggie waste, grass cuttings, shredded fall leaves as well as spent "gift" plants in containers accumulate here and give forth this miracle.

That's when another crystal heart came to light, from the beautiful black composted earth.

Often in live floral arrangements from florists, stones or heart-shaped glass crystals are used at the bottom of containers for draining purposes. When the flowers have expired, the crystals end up with the dead flowers in the composter.

They return as messages, a reminder of love shared and sent, as the floral tribute had been in the beginning.

My clematis is planted, and the new perennials. The months have come and gone. It will be summer again soon and the sun will make my crystal heart glisten, bringing back many fond memories.

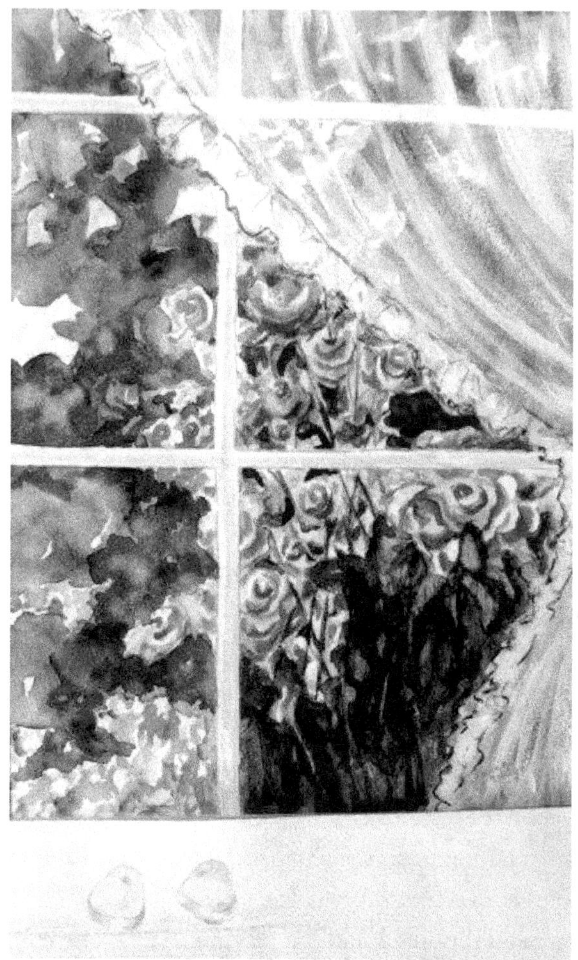

Maureen Mullally's Crystal Hearts watercolour.

Georgeina Knapp - Spirit of the Hills 2019 Short Prose Contest Winner

MRS. MOFFATT'S LAZY DAY

It was almost a year since Mrs. Moffatt and Victoria met. Mrs. Moffatt had needed a place to live and Victoria owned a small, cozy house that would be most suitable for the two of them. The situation soon developed into a comfortable and harmonious routine which both enjoyed.

Today Victoria and Mrs. Moffatt enjoyed their breakfast together as they did every day. Since it was a weekday, Victoria hugged Mrs. Moffatt good-bye and left in her small, blue car heading down the quiet lane toward the village library where she worked.

As she was most days, Mrs. Moffatt was alone in the house. It would have been silent except for the tuneless hum of the dishwasher and the soft music playing on the radio. Mrs. Moffatt went into the living room and headed to her favourite chair. It was a good chair, soft and cozy, covered with a pattern of bright flowers that reminded her of the garden on a summer day. Sitting in the chair she looked out of the window at the garden and felt the welcome spring sunshine on her face. Mrs. Moffatt was at an age where she particularly appreciated the sunshine. She seemed to be neither young nor particularly old and could be described as either approaching or into middle age, the determination depending on whether your personality was of the glass-half-full or half-empty type.

The morning was spent in that fuzzy, half-awake half-asleep state that warm sunshine always causes. Lunch time came, then time for Mrs. Moffatt to do her daily tour of garden inspection. The white picket fence avoided being a cliché by fitting perfectly as a background to the tulips, daffodils, hyacinths, fritillary, and anemones which were exuberantly welcoming spring. The air was scented with the damp earth, grass, and flowers, while the newly returned birds sang in the trees, which were daily unfurling more tender leaves. After examining and inhaling the scent of each type of flower in the gardens, and having consumed her quota of fresh air, Mrs. Moffatt returned to her comfy chair for her afternoon nap.

The sound of Victoria's car turning off the road woke Mrs. Moffatt and she bustled over to the door as she did every day. Victoria came in, hung her coat on the old fashioned hall tree behind the door, and set her book on the small table next to her favourite chair ready for an evening of reading.

Victoria told Mrs. Moffatt about her day at the library while she prepared their dinner of grilled chicken, carrots, and fluffy mashed potatoes, with ice cream for dessert. After enjoying their dinner, the dishes were placed into the dishwasher and it was time to spend a quiet evening together. Victoria sat in her favourite chair and picked up her book. Mrs. Moffatt curled up on her lap; Victoria rubbed her tabby ears and was rewarded with a loud purr. This was the perfect ending to Mrs. Moffatt's lazy day.

Donna Wootton

THE GARDENER

What's left after years of transforming nature
Is the magic his hands created and cultivated
From the pictures in his mind's eye,
Pictures I revisit in albums from trips
To Newfoundland along the Humber River
Where we discovered wind-swept banks
And fishermen singing their own soul songs.

To the Arctic in August where we picked
Cranberries growing low in surprising
Bunches of bright red on the tundra.
To Japan walking along the Nakasendo Path
That meanders between low mountains
Through craft villages a day's hike apart
Where we contemplated landscaped gardens.

The super moon casts its luminous glow
Across snow covered ground where shadows
Take shape in silhouettes forming designs
Worthy of a master gardener at work.
The winter sun warms the cold air and sparkles
A dormant mask of snow to welcome
A glorious day that lifts the spirit.

Yet I do not venture outside under the canopy
But sit alone in reverie soaking up moon shadows
Or basking in a yellow glitter of sunlight.
Were I to plunge deeper how would I feel?
Is the artistry of this riot among the trees enough?
Can I welcome the history of an intimate cultivator?
Or will I drown drawing on stray thoughts?

Richard Marvin Grove

CATCHING UP TO HER

It seems that mother is not ready to go,
which is joyfully fine with me, even though
the longest journey that she currently takes
clutching
is walking to the end of her bed and back.

The black dog of death has been licking
gently at her heels for some time. No pain,
no fear, just a gentle slobbering
as if your black lab was licking
the honey of life from her reluctance to leave.
She does not even know that she should,
could or would want to leave us to feed
that black dog of mortality.

Now, she, the oldest on our family tree
for generations past, I am
slowly catching up to her
as "I ache in the places where I used to play,"
as my idol, now passed, Leonard Cohen,
said in one of his poems.

Even though I will miss my dear mother
when the gentle black dog
inhales her final breath
I am ok with her passing now.

I often say that she, I, we all,
are "only" going to pass on.
After all we are now,
as dead as we are ever going to be.
It is not the worst thing
compared to some of the traumas
of this mortal trapping called life.

Lionel, great grandson, in some
abstract time-veiled way, still
remembers riding on Great Grandma's scooter
beeping the horn of life, filling her
with joy and there he is smiling at eternity
catching up to me. I hope one day
I have a great-grandson that I can remind,
man is neither young nor old
but lives in eternity.

Michael Croucher

THE WHITE TOUCH OF WINTER

Robert McGraw's new brogues left a solitary trail along the sidewalk of St. Johns Road. He tilted his umbrella forward to protect his scarf and tie. When he reached the familiar wide steps, he stopped and breathed deeply, climbed them and entered the building through the main door. A small and sparsely decorated tree, loops of garland and a few Christmas cards adorned the lobby's long reception counter. He looked towards the only person behind it.

The nurse's voice echoed. "She's ready to see you, Mr. McGraw, you can go on down."

"Thank you."

Her door loomed. It was impersonal. Stark. Coldly finite. Robert entered, stopping just short of the bed. He dug deep for some cheer. "Good morning, Mom. You're looking better. More colour than yesterday."

Her eyes were pale rivets in dark bags. They locked onto his face and struggled. "You weren't here yesterday. No one was. None of you come anymore."

"I was..." he started, then caught himself. He remembered the counsellor's words. *Speak from your feelings and offer comfort. Just don't expect much, and understand that trying to correct her will frustrate you both.* "Are you comfortable? Would you like a biscuit and some juice?"

"Last week those buggers from Junction Road took my slippers. The floors are cold here. I want my slippers."

Time for her is a jumble, last month, last year, last decade or even fifty years ago might seem like last night. And the details, well, she'll take them from a kaleidoscope of memories. It's all part of the process, Mr. McGraw.

The lady had given him a booklet. He kept it on his kitchen counter as a constant reference, unmoved for several months.

"I love you Mom." He plumped her pillow, tightened the sheets and kissed her dry forehead.

No response. Her eyes fixed on the door. "Tell them I want my slippers."

Fifteen minutes in the visitor's chair and none of his words reached her. It became clear that this was a day when she wouldn't be lucid and wouldn't comprehend who he was. Her mind was away somewhere, stuck in a maze that was beyond anyone's reach. He stood. "I'll be back tomorrow morning, Mom."

"Brown slippers." Her head dropped onto to the pillow and rolled from side to side. She grimaced, a tear slid down her cheek. "Junction Road…bastards took them."

Through his own tears, McGraw found his coat and left her room. He walked slowly down the hallway to gather his composure. The nurse at reception waved when he passed, he nodded and pushed through the big door. The snow was thicker now, the sidewalk patterned with fresh prints. At the bottom of the steps, he stopped, took a breath and let the cool air ease the tightness in his throat.

During his walk down Runnymede Road to the subway station, his mind was busy sorting through happier images of her. Better times. Christmas lunches and Thanksgiving dinners came to mind. He remembered her delight in preparing them for family and friends, and for the added guests that so often appeared. Sometimes twenty or more people had crowded her tables. His mom loved to share her table.

He shook his head at the injustice. Since she'd become ill, it disgusted him that happy reflections of those times had been taken from her. All things past and present seemed to be lost in the blur of her world, drifting behind a confusing clutter of images and thoughts. A sporadic churchgoer, he wondered about his Maker. *How could He thrust a wonderful and giving woman like his mom mercilessly into an existence like this?*

Cutting deeper as he walked were his own feelings for her. She was the only person in his life who'd shown love for him under all circumstances and through every ordeal. She'd known when to connect, quickly discovering his wants, fears and frustrations. She always found exactly the right words, or read him just the right story. Many years ago, every day for two weeks, they'd sat in the plush rattan chairs of the sunroom. Chapter by chapter, she'd read him *The Secret Garden.* Those sessions had been just the right tonic for the nagging fear he'd had over getting his tonsils removed.

He pictured her pretty smile and its mystical effect on him. He heard her words as she closed the book. *Fear and anger are small demons, Robert. Change your thoughts and you'll chase them away. You'll be fine. Demons out first, then your tonsils. That's what we do all through life, sweetheart. We deal with our problems as they come. We think, rethink, and do what we can. But we can help expel our demons…by making better thoughts.*

The snow fell in big flakes all around him. The memories had been therapeutic. It was better to reminisce this way than at the hospital. His reflections were always devastatingly painful when experienced within sight of her.

The memories drifted away. By the time he'd joined the flow of commuters into the station, he was concentrating on the objectives of his busy day.

A pretty but roughly dressed girl sat on a blanket in the station's concourse. A guitar box sat open beside her, the inside of the lid sprinkled with coins. She was singing a carol, "We Three Kings." She performed it sweetly, but not well. He filed past with the flow of commuters and enjoyed the short diversion that her voice offered. She looked up and smiled when he dropped coins into the lid.

The escalator took him down to the platform level. The girl started another carol, "Silent Night." The lyrics, although distant and muffled, still reached him…*Mother and child…Sleep in heavenly peace…Sleep in heavenly peace…Mother and child…Sleep in heavenly peace.*

It was his mother's favourite carol. He remembered her singing it softly in the kitchen as she baked her Christmas cookies. He closed his eyes and silently gave thanks for the girl's music, embracing the memories it had inspired.

When Robert reopened his eyes, he knew what his mother would want. He moved along the platform area and away from the crowd of commuters. He was drained. His eyes filled up. He sat on a bench that was unoccupied, lowered his head and sobbed shamelessly into the ends of his scarf. Trains came and went in both directions, but he stayed on the bench, face cradled in his palms, content to let time and trains pass him by. The tears stopped coming when he'd dealt with the day's grief. He thought again of better times and better things to come and released more demons.

Rev. Janet Stobie

TWO MOTHERS, TWICE BLESSED

The deeper that sorrow carves into your being,
the more joy you can contain.
(The Prophet, by Kahlil Gibran)

I think I've always known that I was an adopted child. It wasn't until my fifteenth birthday that Mom mustered the courage to tell me the full story of my arrival in our family.

"When your dad and I were first married we shared a house with your Uncle Tom and Aunt Rachel. Children came easily for them, three little boys in five years." Mom paused. She glanced over at her wedding photograph hanging above the mantel. "For your dad and I it wasn't so easy. We waited thirteen years. Like Hannah in the Bible, I begged God for a child: 'Why is Rachel blessed with children and not me?' An emergency hysterectomy when I was thirty-three ended all hope."

Tears dripped down her cheeks. I reached out and wiped them away. "Oh Mom," I said. "I'm sorry."

"It's okay, hon," Mom said as she patted my hand. "This story has a happy ending. We decided we would adopt a child or two. I was so excited when the phone calls finally came." A big smile lit up her face. "The first time our social worker Mrs. Robertson called, she informed us she had a three-month-old baby, a little girl, just for us. Of course, that was your big sister Anne." Mom straightened her back as she looked up at Anne's picture in its ornate frame, sitting right on the mantel. Her eyes turned back to mine. "But we had asked for two children. We told Mrs. Robertson we wanted another girl."

Mom reached out and tenderly brushed away the hair that habitually covered my eyes. As always, her loving touch felt good. "Nearly five years passed before Mrs. Robertson called again. They had another little girl, eighteen months old. I was ecstatic."

I lifted down my picture from the mantel piece and handed it to Mom. Her eyes filled with tears once again, but this time tears of joy. "You were such a cuddly baby, always wanting to be held. I remember that first day so well. We had to pick you up from the hospital. When the nurse brought you out to us, you were sobbing as if your heart was broken. When she handed you to me, you wrapped your little arms around my neck and buried your face in my chest. I knew from that moment you were meant to be my little girl."

Mom reached out to me and I snuggled into her hug. I still love to be held, I thought.

"I love you so much," Mom said. "You have always been my little sunshine. You are truly God's blessing for us."

My heart swelled with love. Adoption was a precious gift for me. Dreams of my birth family were non-existent. My mom and dad loved me. I was special.

In addition to her unconditional love, my adoptive mom gave me the gift of faith. Faith for Mom was not confined to Sunday worship. Every morning, she greeted me from her favourite chair, her Bible open on her lap. Over the years her precious Bible became worn with use. As her eyesight grew dim, I replaced it with a large-print edition. She hardly needed the new one. She had learned so many passages by heart. I believe my journey to ordained ministry began with my mother's faithful example.

Twenty years ago, on a Friday afternoon, Mom fell and broke her hip. She was ninety. Two days later, the surgery over, I sat with Mom in intensive care. Small and fragile, she almost disappeared in the hospital bed. Her eyes glistened with tears, as she said, "You've filled my life with joy, Janet. I'm so proud you're my daughter."

"I love you," I answered. "You're my wonderful mom." I held her hand, afraid that a hug would hurt her. We sat in silence, listening to the machines that were monitoring Mom's heart and blood pressure. Several hours later, that hospital room became holy ground when my adopted sister Anne and I held Mom as death quietly overtook her being. At that most sacred moment, I knew in the depth of my soul that God had acted through adoption to bring goodness for both of us. Thirteen years of aching for a family had carved a deep well of sorrow in Mom's life. Adoption had filled that well with love and joy.

After the funeral, I found my adoption papers in Mom's safety deposit box. With shaking fingers, I unfolded this flimsy bridge to my past. My birth name, Sharon Margaret, stared back at me. I had a new identity.

I spoke my name into the emptiness of the room, listened to its sound, felt its shape on my tongue. Is that me? Do I want to be this mystery person? Grief for my adoptive mom overwhelmed me. I refolded the papers and tucked them into my purse. I don't need this information, I thought. Back home, I filed the papers carefully away and carried on with my life. That door was closed.

A year later, I confided to my friend Carol, "Doctors keep asking if diabetes or heart disease run in my family. I think I'd like to find my birth parents and get some medical history."

Carol jumped in immediately, "If you know your birth name, we can search for it on Canada 411. You were born in London. We'll search southwestern Ontario. Back then, Children's Aid looked for adoptive parents near the child's birth place. This will be an adventure."

I wasn't so sure, but I let Carol try. The search yielded only fifty-two matches for my birth surname. I drafted a form letter, identifying myself as Reverend Janet Stobie, writing on behalf of Sharon Margaret. My mind whirling with guilt, anxiety and hope, I shoved those letters into the mailbox. "No matter what comes of this, I'll always love you," I whispered to my adoptive mom. As I walked away, I reasoned with my guilt, telling myself that Mom wouldn't mind. She'd offered to give us our birth names several times. Always we refused. "This is not betrayal. Besides, I probably won't hear anything anyway."

Within two weeks, I received a reply. I stared at the London postmark, afraid to open it. I laid the envelope on the kitchen table while I brewed a cup of tea. It's time, I thought. Open it, Janet. You *do* want to know. A whiff of rose perfume wafted past my nose as I unfolded the very feminine notepaper and began to read:

Dear Rev. Stobie, I remember some hushed talk about a child born to my husband's sister many years ago. There could be a connection, but I don't know for sure. Ivan died two months ago, so I can't ask him. Do you have any more information?
Sincerely, Sarah Grigg

With scant hope, I typed out a reply:

Dear Mrs. Grigg, Thank you so much for answering my letter. I offer my sympathy in the death of your husband. Sharon's adoption papers say that her mother was sixteen. She was unmarried and worked as a waitress. That's all the information we have. Once again, I thank you for your interest.
Blessings, Rev. Janet.

To my surprise, several weeks later I received a second response. This time, the message came as an email:

Dear Rev. Stobie, two weeks ago my wife received your letter from her sister-in-law Sarah. Why is Sharon searching for her birth mom? I look forward to hearing from you.
Sincerely, Sam.

We exchanged several cautious emails before Sam wrote, "I think mother should talk with daughter. Please have Sharon Margaret write to her mom."

I dropped my façade and sent a letter. My email was formal and stilted, but it was enough. My birth mom answered. I had found her, that simply. Aunt Sarah had forwarded my letter to her. She lived in Arizona and was coming to Canada in the fall. We set up a meeting at a hotel in Niagara Falls. The deed was done. The contact was made.

Over the next three months, I worried. I dreamed. I prayed. What would she be like? Do I look like her? Why is she willing to see me? Is this a foolish adventure? I prayed some more.

My birth mom reserved a hotel room in Niagara Falls for my daughter and me. When we checked in, a pile of gaily wrapped gifts greeted us. A tiny white stuffed lamb gazed up at us from the top of the pile. As soon as my fingers touched its softness, my tears began to pour. All the pain and fear of the abandoned child I had once been enveloped me. I was so grateful my daughter, Connie, a busy working mom herself, was with me. I needed her. She held me until my sobs lessened. Then we talked for hours, about my adoptive mom, my fears in meeting my birth mom, about being mothers ourselves. Eventually, peace descended. We slept.

My heart pounded as I walked into the hotel lobby at ten o'clock the next morning. An older version of myself stepped forward from a group of four women and reached out to give me a hug. "Now, we're not going to cry," she whispered in my ear. But of course, we did. Tears silently slipped down both our cheeks. Already I knew this slim, stylishly dressed woman was my birth mom. She looked like me, sounded like me, even walked like me. Never had I resembled anyone. I felt I had come home.

Overwhelmed by emotion, I became that bewildered, frightened baby in my adoptive mom's story. I desperately wanted to climb into my birth mom's lap and sob on her shoulder. This was my mom, and I was terrified I would lose her again. I clung to her hand as she led my daughter and me to her three sisters.

The introductions over, we settled into chairs in the atrium. Mom opened with, "Tell me about your life." As I talked, her face relaxed and her shoulders straightened as her guilt visibly fell away. Several times she interrupted with, "You had the life you deserved…you had the life you deserved." This, too, was a most sacred time. Her total acceptance and love and that of her sisters overwhelmed me. I had two moms. Very different people, yet they both loved me, and I loved them both.

The six of us had two days together. As my daughter and I were leaving, my birth mom said, "We won't say goodbye. I don't like goodbyes. You'll come to visit. March is a good month in Arizona."

"Yes," I responded. "Of course, I'll come. I can't let go of you again." We set our plans, hugged some more, and left.

During the second of what came to be my yearly visits to Arizona, I gathered my courage and asked Mom to tell me my story. I chose an evening, after my stepfather had gone to bed. The silent house kept watch and listened as my mom opened her heart's door to let me in.

"Your father was a sailor," she said. "We didn't have long together. He left on his ship and didn't return. It's too painful to remember him, but I'll tell you about you and me. I was sixteen when you were born. Having a baby out of wedlock was a terrible thing in those days. The entire family felt my shame, but I brought you home anyway. I couldn't let you go. I was going to raise you myself, no matter what. My two brothers and three sisters were thrilled with you. You were *our baby*. For fifteen months, we all loved you."

She fell silent, her pain overwhelming her. She shook her head, took a deep breath and continued. "If I could have stayed home and cared for you, maybe everything would have worked out. I don't know. The bottom line was, I had to work at the restaurant." She raked her fingers through her hair. "Dad made very little money, and drank most of that. Until some of us were old enough to get a job, we often went hungry.

Life was difficult…horrible." She shivered. "One night, I came home from work. You weren't in your crib. I searched the house and found you sobbing quietly in the corner of 'that room.' For years, my father had been abusing me in 'that room.' As a child, I learned not to cry because the abuse was worse when I cried." Her shoulders slumped, her face pale, Mom looked abused. I watched her clench her teeth and take several deep breaths. "That night, I was sure he had started on you. I couldn't protect you when I wasn't home. I had no choice. I wanted you to be safe, free from the fear and the pain that I lived. I called the Children's Aid the next morning and told them it wasn't safe for you to be with me. They came and took you away. We were all heartbroken."

Mom reached out and touched my cheek. Her clear blue eyes were dark with pain.

"I trusted you would be safe," she continued. "They promised to find a good home for you. I had to believe them. There was nothing else I could do. When the car drove away, I closed the door of my heart to the pain and made my brothers and sisters promise never to speak of you again. It was the only way I could survive."

She fell silent. Her eyes glistened with tears, but only a few drops seeped out and down her cheeks. She didn't ask my forgiveness.

"You've had the life you deserved. You were safe and loved." She whispered the words.

"Yes," I replied. "I've had a good life."

Mom smiled through her tears. "Thank you."

I reached out with a hug, another most sacred moment.

As a mother, I have always believed it is my privilege and responsibility to protect my children. Mom paid the ultimate sacrifice to protect me. She gave me away into safe and loving hands. Although she declared she had closed the door on that part of her life, she named my younger half-sister Sharon Janet. I know in my heart that I was never forgotten, always loved.

For twelve wonderful years I was welcomed and loved as a full family member by Mom, Sam, and my three wonderful half-sisters. Six years ago, I spent six weeks in Arizona. For Mom, they were six weeks of excruciating physical pain as she battled the last stages of cancer. For me, they were six weeks of sleepless nights and days. I held her as her body shook with pain, read to her as she tried to sleep, held the pink bowl as she vomited every few hours, a side effect of the useless pain medication. Yet, they were six precious weeks for both of us. There were no closed doors between us. We laughed at funny movies. We shared memories of past accomplishments, failures, fun. We were mother and daughter, loving and solid. Our love gave her strength. We prayed together, for she too was a woman of faith. She didn't attend a church, but she knew God.

At her memorial service, I talked of my birth mom's amazing emotional strength, her ramrod straight back, her love for her four daughters.

I loved her as I loved my adoptive mom. Together they gave me life, values, and faith. Yes, sorrow carved a deep bowl into each of us, a bowl that later overflowed with joy, faith, and love. I strive to be like both of my moms, strong, faithful, a blessing for the world. Unlike most people, I have been loved by two mothers. I am truly twice blessed.

Kim Aubrey

THE MOTHERS

This winter the mothers died—
Mary who held herself and her family
together, Ruth who taught them to receive,
Janet's mum who forgot how to live—
leaving husbands, daughters, sons
to grieve.

Moms who used to bake, take care
of grandkids, cater to their men
women whom illness has beached
whales with a need to be watered keen
not for themselves but for loved ones
all at sea

who languish without their daily cups
of care, mothers whose hands shake unused
to taking, whose faces crumple as they lie
in unmade beds and yearn to rise
sweep the hardwood, slice onions
for home-fries.

My own mom released after surgery wakes
before dawn, dresses for Christmas, cuts
grapefruit, cleans glasses we left in the sink,
hovers as I lift the twenty-pound bird—her call
for six—hands primed, always ready to help, or to hold.

Linda Hutsell-Manning

THE CALF IN HIDDEN VALLEY

seeing you again that *how are you old friend*
those clichéd phrases still the best
we dally over coffee paint the spaces where we last left off
our lives now so divergent town and country mouse
each of us freed for these two days
to drift and cradle our forgotten lives

I spin out Hidden Valley discovered by my children
off on forays through the pastures to a wild
forgotten place home to our neighbour's cattle
ringed on one side by an unattended forest
giant mossy logs dead branches pick-up-stick and tangled
its secret path along the remnant of an access road that
winds past sagging page wire fences
guarding apple trees all Bonsai twisted in the wind

you hesitate
your smooth-soled shoes unused to tramping
out through fields down unmarked trails
I praise the valley's spirit
how it breathes a stillness calms the mind
a shimmering utopia especially in the spring

we climb the hill behind our house
through blades of grass reaching up between
the criss-cross husks of last year's growth

along the ridge where rows of
new green corn sprouts curl to drink the dew
down a narrow tangled path
avoiding poison ivy past the tissue paper trilliums
into apple blossom air alive with love-drugged
reckless birds all trilling for a mate

we breathe in musky morning air
hear water gurgling from the steep-banked creek
a giant valley boa twisting from the hills of
old Northumberland out to the distant lake
I plan to take you to the spot where our son David
found the footprint of a house indented in the boggy river bank
spent hours digging treasures from its silent grassy grave
a massive branch-twined lilac radiating scent and long
forgotten plans as each small artifact appeared
just past the stream's first twist green ruff of water cress
telltale ripples of a fish now hiding in sun-mottled rocks
we hear a bawling high-pitched frantic
racing up the knoll then down to where a finger
of the creek exuberant in early spring has channelled
out a gaping crevice underneath a fallen tree
we see a half grown calf that flails and slams
erratically against the branches body sleek with sweat
and blood the herd a distance off one cow
perhaps its mother answers mournfully
her lowing an intermittent melancholy dirge

when we appear the calf intensifies its thrashing
fresh blood spurting from one mud-soaked ear
foam from its bawling mouth tinged pink its eyes
rolled back the last instinctive frenzied push
for freedom or for death

you watch your eyes almost as frightened
as the calf's while I approach heart pounding
calling gently reaching for its head resistance
terror as it bawls again I slip and grab a branch
you call me beg for reason still I try once more
knowing if we leave it won't survive
I hold its head sing lullabies old nursery rhymes
as breath by laboured breath it calms is still
we need a rope more hands you'll stay?
a test of more than friendship as you kneel
beside me touch the creature's bloodied face

I run ignoring creek bed poison ivy branches
storm the house wake daughter Laura
grab a coil of rope *you'll never visit me again*

we find you sitting one hand on its foam-soaked face
we're doing fine it's hardly moved
I show the calf the rope explain stand ankle deep
in dung-sprayed mud arrange the loop smell fear
and hope to God we three can pull it out three women
digging in our heels reluctant midwives straining
on the rope to pull this blood-soaked bawling calf
thrashing from its muddy womb

we watch it stumble out escape the rope and us
its mother's strong insistent voice the calf replies
then in slow motion stops to turn give us a long unblinking stare
soft hairs along its muzzle backlit by the sun a twitch and wildness
reappears it wheels round trots self-assured back to its former life.

Christopher Cameron

THE SIRENS OF WISHEMAGOG

The four women were at Fan's summer cottage for three days of bridge, drinking, and swimming. They played cards deep into each evening, stopping only when some or all of them were too inebriated to go on. On the second night, as their boozy session ended and the losers were fetching the final round from the knotty pine kitchen, Fan had suggested a pre-sunrise swim.

"The water is incredibly warm this year. It'll be heaven at dawn."

Almost every day that summer, the garish Fahrenheit thermometer Fan's mother had hung up decades ago had hovered around the 80-degree mark. The hot weather made the lake water warm and comforting. Amniotic.

"And we'll go commando," said Lex, holding a bowl of ice cubes. "The best way to swim. The only way."

They stared at her.

"Commando," she repeated. "Naked."

More staring.

"That's not what commando means," said Fan, a professor.

"Well it should. Whatever. There has to be a better term than skinny dipping. It sounds like giggling ten-year-olds at summer camp." Lex hated giggling at any age.

"Fine with me," said Fan. "I do it all the time here."

"I could go," said Nobie, "if everybody else is."

"I'll join you," said Barbara. "But I'm wearing a suit."

"No you're not," said Lex. "Barenaked ladies only."

"*If I had a million dollars. . .*" sang Fan.

"You do," said Nobie. Fan's divorce settlement was a topic endlessly discussed by everyone except her.

They knew Barbara would eventually agree to join them. She had a habit of never committing to anything until she had reviewed all the other possibilities.

"It will be a bonding experience." Lex was motivating them, as she always did.

"Bonding? Isn't that what men do?" asked Fan. "Hunting, fishing, peeing in the snow?"

"Well, what do we do?"

Fan thought. "We share," she said, drawing out the word.

"We could pee in the lake," Nobie offered.

"Not helpful."

"People do not stare at groups of naked men through binoculars," said Barbara, who had been silent.

"Speak for yourself," said Fan.

"You mean like some old guy in a plaid shirt sitting on his dock?" This was Nobie.

"Wear your towel until you get into the water," said Lex. "Then drop it and dive in. You're a smart lady. You'll figure it out. Take charge of your own nudity, woman."

"Keep in mind," said Fan, "that we are several decades beyond being prime peeping-Tom material. Anyone in a plaid shirt would probably swing his binoculars away and look for stray loons."

"Jesus, if we were men, this wouldn't even be a thing," Lex noted. "We'd just go down to the lake and swim. But *we* have to plan it as if it were the Invasion of Normandy."

"Commando style!" barked Nobie. "We meet at oh-six-hundred."

"That's when we fall in?" Drunken laughter.

"We can swim out to the rock. Be sirens," said Lex.

A smooth, dark rock rose from the water about fifty metres off the end of the cottage dock. There were places to sit or stand on its underwater ledges with just your head and shoulders showing.

"I don't know if I can swim that far," said Nobie. "Are there water wings?"

"You don't need water wings." Lex was looking at Nobie's chest. "You'll get plenty of flotation from those things."

Nobie had gotten the implants years ago, demanded and paid for by her husband. They were all the more noticeable because the rest of her was so petite. Everybody including Nobie thought they looked ridiculous. She was always talking about getting rid of them.

A little more drunken laughter and then bed.

***

What am I doing here? Nobie wondered, as the warm pre-dawn gloom enveloped her. Standing here with waves lapping at my bottom. She stole a look at the others; they were so well proportioned, smooth skin, muscles even. She knew that she alone evidenced a lifetime of children, banana bread, and fake boobs. A beer-can body with giant jugs.

So much of her had become unimportant, it seemed. She had been a decent student in high school, a cheerleader, a lifeguard even. None of that had meant anything after she married. From the beginning Mike treated her as he would a slightly dimwitted waitress. Decades later, she hardly existed; teased by her grown-up children and viewed with condescending possessiveness by her spouse.

A friend had once helped her set up her own email account, but her husband had made her take it down. "What reason does a married couple have to keep secrets from each other?" he'd asked.

"As if he has no secrets from you," one of her friends had snorted. "Christ, Nobie, sometimes…" Nobie knew everybody knew more than she did about her husband. But she let it go. She was a person of faith, and that included faith that things would work out.

99

And they did. One night he was gone, taken by an unexpected and final heart attack apparently brought on by a lot of alcohol; discovered by Nobie in a hotel room along with lingering traces of some other woman, who had wisely fled. Her first thought after she found him had been that she would never again have to worry about saying or doing something stupid. Even so, she knew there were details of that night that she would never share with anyone. Some things were private.

Nobie watched Barbara's straight back get shorter and shorter as she walked into the water just ahead. It was amazing how pale her skin was. Like flour. Beautiful in a way, almost ghostlike.

She looked down at her own skin disappearing into the green-grey water. Nothing to see here, folks. Move along. And she plunged in.

When she swung her arms to swim, she found her breasts wanted to move in the opposite direction from the rest of her. That's it, she thought. These stupid things are going as soon as I get back home. I don't care if I'm scarred for life.

She lifted her head out of the water and peered across the lake to see if the man in the plaid shirt was anywhere about.

***

They all knew this was not her, Barbara thought, taking another step into the water and pulling the hem of the towel higher so it wouldn't get wet. She wasn't really scanning the far shore looking for a man with binoculars. But she knew the others thought she was.

She unfastened her towel and slid it onto the dock. Walking quickly into the water she looked down at her skin glowing in the early morning light. A boyfriend had once called it alabaster. Fish-belly white another one had. She felt the water tickle up her body as she waded deeper. There was a quiet swish to her right as Nobie swam past.

Oh heck, she thought, and dove in, spreading her arms wide to gather the lake around and cover herself. There was a sudden, extraordinary sensation of water absolutely everywhere, stroking her skin

100

in all places at the same instant, exploring her. An unfamiliar feeling, but not unpleasant.

"I'm not sure I want anything to know me as well as you seem to," she said to the water playing in and around her mouth. This wasn't something she would easily get used to.

Fan, Lex, and Nobie were all swimming ahead of her. It had taken her a while after meeting them to realize that these were nicknames for Frances, Alexandra, and Zenobia (a stupid name my hippie parents gave me, Nobie said). Barbara had always been Barbara.

She looked ahead at her friends as they swam towards the rock. Can they tell? Can they see from my eyes what I have seen? By looking at me, can they see where his hands have been?

The affair had shocked her with its suddenness and intensity. Their first meeting had taken place at their church choir practice, of all places. He was new and didn't seem to know anyone there. One evening for some reason she never learned, he had taken an interest in her and so she took an interest back. On their third coffee date he looked straight into her eyes and said, "What I'd really like is to lie next to you somewhere. So close that a butter knife couldn't fit between us. And for you to tell me what you love, who your heroes are, what you dream about, and what you want from your life."

Later that night in her carefully decorated apartment, when she had found herself in actual closeness with him, she hadn't been able to think of anything to say in answer to any of it. But at that point it seemed not to matter. In the six months they were together, they learned little more about each other than their names and their bodies.

Barbara normally clung to familiarity and she knew it, but intimacy with him took her to a new place between discovery and oblivion. As he quickened above her she would wait for his climax and sprint toward her own, which she clawed and grasped to reach.

"You have a euphemism for all occasions don't you?" he had said—not teasing, just in wonder—when she confided that in her mind she had always called it a "shiver." She knew perfectly well what the sensation was supposed to be called, but she was uncomfortable using base or clinical terms when there were so many more pleasant ways of saying things.

On the night it ended, six weeks ago, she couldn't decide whether she was devastated that it was over or relieved to be free of wondering when it would be. There was no doubt that part of her would miss what she'd come to think of as their butter-knife closeness.

Barbara ducked her head down and swam underwater for as long as she could, kicking her legs furiously, wanting no part of her to be missed by the lake. Splashing into the air, she held her breath for a second and then exhaled with a soft, surprised squeak.

"Barbara, are you cold already?" asked Fan.

"Just a little shiver," she said.

***

Lex tossed her towel onto the dock and walked straight to the water without pausing. She dove smoothly in and began swimming, arms lifting upward with every stroke, like wings.

When they had all assembled at the rock she announced, "Okay folks, the Tuesday morning ladies' swimming gala is officially underway. Please adjust your bathing costumes."

"We came, we stripped, we swam," burbled Nobie, treading water.

They found rock ledges to sit on that kept the water at collarbone level.

Of all of them Lex most loved the life she had. Right out of university she had strode into a brilliant career in marketing followed by a bestselling series of self-help books for businesswomen. She truly believed the things she wrote—I am independent and successful, she often thought, and I have achieved my ideal self. My mission now is to help others do the same. Take yourself seriously, she told the women in her seminars. No one will if you don't. If you take that first step, you can achieve anything.

She pulled herself up onto the wet rock and draped herself over it, arms over her head, letting the water form a skirt around her hips.

"Okay, sailors, here I am."

"What is that bruise?" asked Nobie, looking at Lex's left side.

Lex glanced down. "My doubles partner whacked me accidentally with his tennis racket the other day." This was partly accurate: it was her partner, but it wasn't a tennis racket and it wasn't accidental.

But Lex slid slowly back in to the water to hide the bruise, sighing a little as the rough surface of the rock abraded her skin.

"We won't tell anyone about this will we?" Barbara asked.

"Good God, you make it sound like we're robbing a casino or something," said Lex, but she used her seminar voice, trying hard to be gentle.

They were quiet for few moments.

Lex usually found her short-term lovers when she was away from her husband on business, roping them out of the corral of the hotel bar—if there was another use for a hotel bar she couldn't imagine what. She never justified the roughness she looked for, which was always confidential and almost always consensual. She simply found it easier to reach a sexual conclusion that way. Most of her choices went along; some fled; a recent one had even passed out drunk, ending her evening early.

Nobie's voice cut through the stillness.

"Where's Fan?"

✳✳✳

They had walked under the silent pine trees in the pre-dawn, a tiny flashlight showing them where to step along the flagstone path to the lake. When they got to the water Fan waded right in, feeling like she was putting on the most comfortable outfit she had ever owned. She stroked easily away from shore, following Lex, who had slipped in first, like a racing sloop being launched.

Fan had spent her childhood summers splashing in this lake and building forts in the trees, and her adolescence Scotch-taping photos from movie magazines to the pine walls of her cottage bedroom. Years later, as she had always dreamed of doing, she and her husband brought their own children for vacations, before they started going to camp and eventually staying home to work at their summer jobs. As they grew up they found excuses not to come, and she realized that they had never felt the same as she did about the place. For Fan, the lake was always here, the one constant in her life. Its name, Wishemagog, was one of those typical English perversions of an Indigenous place name. As a pre-teen she had named it Wish-I-Might. Her children called it Lake Washing Machine.

I do love these women, Fan thought, as she watched her three friends strung out across the short distance to the rock, parting the lake mist with their strokes. We are one, commingled by the cup of the water.

As a wronged ex-wife Fan had been a failure. Her friends all assumed that she had gotten a huge settlement from her husband when she divorced him, considering he'd admitted to at least one affair. But he finessed her out of almost everything, and she had let him. At the last minute he'd acquired some distasteful leverage and she'd buckled under the pressure. Basically the cottage was all she had, along with her condo in Lockport.

A wearying sadness had engulfed her lately, one that came from a deeper, wider source than just her deceased marriage. Existential crisis, she might call it if she used that type of hackneyed language. All her life she'd felt she'd been working towards something—family, people, work, security, home—only to find out the rules had changed. That she should have been heading towards something else. *Do I have the energy to change course? What is there to push off from?*

When the conversation lulled, she swam a little away from the rock and allowed herself to sink into the water. This was a thing she had been doing since she was a teenager—just dropping deeper and deeper, clearing the pressure from her ears as she went, until she knew she had to surface or drown. I could just stay down here, she thought, with no need to breathe, nothing in front of me or behind me.

Wish I might.

She became aware of how deep she was and looked up. Reaching for the silver surface above her head she began to swim toward it. She felt a small stab of panic as it seemed not to be getting any closer. She kicked harder but there was a weakening in her legs and arms, a greying of her vision. The last thing she felt was a sensation like a belt tightening around her chest.

***

The two women broke the surface in a shower of spray.

"I'm all right," Fan coughed, breathing in raggedly. "I'm all right."

"Are you sure?" Nobie had one arm around her.

Fan was aware of Nobie's body against her back, her breasts wet and rubbery, mushing into her, their legs fighting for the same waterspace. Nobie let go and the lake separated them.

"Sorry for grabbing you," Nobie said between breaths. "You were down so long. I wondered if you were all right. I could hardly see you."

"Thank you," Fan croaked in a water-burned voice. "For wondering—"

"Nobie, I didn't know you could dive like that," Lex said. "Well done. You surprise me."

"That makes two of us," Nobie said, still breathless.

Quiet laughter.

"It's starting to get light," said Fan. "We should go back."

And slowly they started swimming under the indigo sky, their wet hair glinting in the strengthening light. The dark green of the water rippling in a freshening breeze made their pale bodies shimmer and dance beneath them. Joined forever by the water they shared, yet each one carrying her secret like a rescued sailor, they moved in unison across their ocean of undiscovered truths.

Untitled by Ted Amsden

Richard Marvin Grove

BOTTLE OF SCOTCH TALKING

It was the Canada Day long weekend at the cottage. The wives, girlfriends and kids were already down for the night. The men, Dan, Mark, Harrison, Bobby and Jimmy, sat around a bonfire mulling over the meaning of life. A bottle of Scotch made its way around the circle three or four times in ponderous silence when Jimmy abruptly broke the spell with slurred words.

"Fuck man, it's not like you can help what fucking family you are born into and how fucked up you are going to get or who is going to fuck with your brain while you are growing up. Did you know that good old fucking Uncle Wally tried fucking with me when I was just little? He tried to get me to give him a blow job when I was about ten or eleven. He was drunk and waggin' his dick in the bushes taking a piss behind the cottage at the edge of the farmer's field. He called me a sissy boy and one day I would have a man's dick like his. He wagged it at me with a grin and said I should give it a suck."

Everyone just sat there in stupefied silence. Harrison finally broke the silence. "Jimmy, is that just the bottle talking man? What are you doing making up stories like that after all these years?"

Jimmy pressed the bottle to his lips and took another swig. "Yah it's the Scotch talkin' but it's all true. I just stood there stunned shivering because I just got out of the lake and I was looking for my towel on the clothesline. He stopped pissing and pointed his manhood at me and dared me to touch it and come into the garage with him. He taunted me and started to walk towards the garage waving to me to follow. As soon as he moved away I grabbed my towel from the clothesline and I ran away. Later he grabbed me by the hair and told me that if I told anyone what he said that he would cut off my nuts and turn me into a girl. I never told no one until this moment. He's an old man now and I finally figured out I don't have to be scared of him no more."

Bobby leaned over Harrison for the bottle of Scotch and took a long swig. "Uncle Wally did the same thing to me one year at the cottage. Who knows, maybe it was the same year or even the same weekend. He grabbed my dick a few times when we were swimming. He laughed and I laughed and he made it funny like it was a joke between friends and then later he cornered me in the garage like he did with you Jimmy. He pulled his wiener out and had me touch it to jerk him off." Bobby took another swig. "He said he wouldn't tell anyone and he would buy me something special and what did I want?" Bobby took another quick swig. "He grabbed my hand and stuck it on his dick. I jerked him a few times and then heard a noise outside so I ran away. Just like you Jimmy, I never told anyone either, till now. From then on I just steered clear of him. Aunt Theresa always said he was a pervert and told the girls to say away from him. She should have told the boys as well."

"He was a classic sexual predator. I was wise to him. He was always scoping out someone to feel up," Harrison said as he reached for the bottle, wiped the spout with his sleeve as he took a quick swig.

Mark leaned forward, "What do you mean he was a sexual predator? I don't think that I even know what a sexual predator is." Mark put air quotes around the words "sexual predator." "Those are pretty loaded words." Mark pulled out his cell phone and started to google. "It says here that: *A sexual predator is a person seen as obtaining or trying to obtain sexual contact with another person in a metaphorically 'predatory' or abusive manner. Analogous to how a predator hunts down its prey.* So that means that the sexual predator is thought to 'hunt' for his or her sex partners. It seems weird that someone would actually hunt down their prey."

"There is nothing weird about it," Harrison said waving the bottle at Mark. "He sussed both of you guys out over time and tried to gain your trust. He even used being half drunk and joking with you as part of his hunting strategy. He went from friendly jokes to trying to get you cornered in the garage. You just had no idea of how long he had been planning his attack. I wonder who he did get jerked off by. You can bet he didn't try it on with just you two. What a fucker."

Mark piped up and read more. The dim blue light of his phone glowed in his scowled face.

Sexual offenders recruit children by establishing a trusting relationship, for example spending time with them and listening to them. They may treat the child as "special"; giving them presents and compliments. Offenders also use gifts and trickery to manipulate and silence the child into keeping the sexual assault a secret. This treatment can isolate the child from siblings, friends or parents. The offender may also establish a trusting relationship with the family and friends of a child, in order to have access to the child alone. When they have obtained the trust of the child and family it makes it much easier for the offender to sexually abuse the child. It is also important to remember that the offender often grooms the family in similar ways by buying gifts or helping out around the house as a way to gain trust from the family.

"There is loads more if you want to look it up but I figure you are all too drunk to care at the moment."

Jim poured another two-finger shot into his glass, took a swig from the bottle and passed it to Mark. Mark sat in silence remembering just how much further Uncle Wally managed to go with him. He choked on his all too vivid memory. Scotch dribbled down his chin as he pulled the bottle from his lips. He was trying to remember what the present was that Uncle Wally gave him for his silence.

"Mark, you must have had a fucked-up moment or two in your life. Didn't everyone? Didn't you tell me years ago that some sexy woman down the street, that you did gardening for, tried to fuck you or something? You used to call her your Mrs. Robinson. How many times did she actually get in your pants?" Mark shrank further into silence. The shame of his Uncle Wally experience swirled through his Scotch-filled mind.

Dan snatched the bottle from Mark and taunted him with a high-pitched childish voice. "Poor Marky got fucked by the lady down the street when he was just fourteen, poor little Marky. Nothing even half as good as that ever happened to me. I saw my big sister standing in her bra and panties one time when I was about fourteen. I hesitated just long enough at her bedroom door, just open a crack, to get a good look and I went into the bathroom and pulled my wire. That's as close as I ever got to pre-pubescent sex. I was stuck with my virginity until I was about twenty-three."

Mark seized the silent moment to stand up. "I don't know about you guys but I'm going to bed." He dragged himself up by the trunk of the tree he was leaning on, turned toward the long grass and peed. Staggering in silence, feet pressing into the cool sand, head swimming in Scotch-filled memories of Uncle Wally as a successful hunter pinning him against the work bench in the garage. Eyes drooping he waved good night.

Shane Joseph

THE FIRE OF LOVE

He woke early, not to the sound of birds, but to the sound of the TV blaring in the living room. He groaned, rolled over, and checked his iPhone. Five o'clock. Why the hell was the TV on at this time of the morning?

The new day rushed at him, not with the promise of fresh experiences to embroider life's tapestry, but with the certainty of an ending created by grievances and hurts, the resentment accumulated like a sludge that wouldn't wash away. How had it gathered mass over time, like a slow oil leak in a car that builds to an indelible stain and ruins a driveway? He pulled the covers over his head and tried to return to sleep, dreading what he had to do today. But the drone from the television was like an accusing bell tolling for him to wake and accept reality.

He rose and pulled on his dressing gown. Through the connecting door into the next bedroom he saw her empty bed; crumpled sheets, blankets and pillows thrown about at random, some on the floor. Underwear that had once awoken his libido lay strewn on a chair. An empty glass with brown residue sat on the bedside table, adjacent to an ashtray piled with cigarette butts. He opened a window in her room and diffused some of the stale tobacco stench. That's why he had a fan running in his room continuously. Cigarettes were not the only reason they slept apart.

He peeped into the living room. Ah, the Royal Wedding. That explained the television. Overdressed celebrities were entering a gothic church, cameras hovering over their elegant clothes and glossy hairstyles; the celebrities themselves were basking in the glow of attention that would be twittering across the world simultaneously on millions of cell phones. He didn't need to watch another bloody wedding. Not today of all days.

She was slouched in front of the goggle box in her white dressing gown, which had turned a dirty cream over the course of their marriage. The bottle of Scotch and another glass resembling the one in her bedroom with the same coloured residue reposed beside it. A tissue box sat beside the bottle, and bundled up tissues littered the floor in front of her lounger.

He went into the kitchen and put on the kettle. Last night's dishes were in the sink, their contents hardening and beginning to smell. Out of habit, he washed the dishes and put them to dry while the coffee brewed. He poured himself a cup, black, and wondered whether to escape into his room, lock the door, and bury himself in some unimportant work—his familiar routine, even on weekends. But this long weekend would be different. He was glad that his suitcases had left yesterday, deposited in the other apartment while she was at work. He would have the next three days to set himself up in his new digs. He had picked the day well, except for this bloody wedding on television that the whole world seemed to be watching. The wedding drew him too.

The bride was entering the nave of the church—alone. His wife had been like that at their wedding ten years ago, herself the product of a broken family whose parents refused to be seen in each other's company; so the mother had shown up for the wedding while the father had gone fishing. As there was no one to "give her away," she had walked up the aisle alone. For him, she said, every time they had quarrelled since. *For him.* Now the royal bride was doing the same, but her stunning gown and practiced walk made her performance all that more important, like a fashion model on a catwalk; having a man by her side would spoil the image. Halfway, a man *did* intervene and spoil things: the bridegroom's stooped father stepped up gallantly and extended his arm. It was boring and normal after that.

Yet, he was intrigued by this wedding. Somehow it looked different. The church was smaller, less opulent than Westminster; the audience comprised entertainment industry glitterati contrasting with the boring royal family in their odd-shaped hats, some that looked like food trays or broken-away parts of foam mattresses; there were no politicians. There were white *and* black guests, just like the couple who were white and black. *Like us!*

He sat in the second lounger facing the television set, one rarely used these days as he preferred to watch TV on his laptop in his room, alone. He sensed her glancing at him, but he did not look in her direction. Silences were to be preserved for as long as possible. They were safe when cocooned in silence.

He had presumed too soon.

"They are a lovely couple," she said, her voice raspy and nasal from crying.

"Hmm."

They had been a lovely couple too. Once. He remembered the tuxedo he had paid a fortune for and gone through many fittings for at the exclusive men's tailor in the city. He had paid with optimism more than cash. After all, he was building a new life. He had even bought the sprawling house in the suburbs, with its empty bedrooms never to be filled with the children of their dreams. Then, he had been an upcoming star in the financial firmament. He traded millions of dollars in a day. Yes, he sometimes lost a couple of million too, but he more than made up his losses the next day. Trading was infectious, better than drugs; it kept him on a high most of the time, except on the days he lost. On those days, the crushing defeat was hard to bear, taken out usually on the one nearest to him—her.

He had met her at a cocktail lounge, the new hostess, brown-skinned, exotic, a struggling actress who was on the tip of stardom, she had told him. Could he introduce her to some of the high rollers he wined and dined most days? Her vulnerability had invoked his lust for conquest, raising it to a peak. They had sex for the first time leaning against his car in the dark parking lot, too frenzied to wait until they got to his condo. They had more sex in the condo afterwards. Sex became a drug like stock trading, until passion waned.

He introduced her selectively to his contacts in the movie industry, but nothing panned out. One producer had asked to sleep with her and she refused. He hadn't introduced her to anyone again.

"Do you remember the dress I wore?"

"Yes." No, he couldn't remember the detail, except that it was white. *Pray, let her not probe me any further.*

"What's so different between them and us?" she continued.

"Money. And ten years."

"We had money." *Once. But when the fall came I lost more than a couple of million in a day, and never recovered.*

"They are too big to fail," he said, wishing she would shut up. The droning white Anglican archbishop shut up instead, and the all-white choir started their mechanically perfect singing, songs that came from the songbook not from the heart.

She reached for her glass, surveyed the contents, wrinkled her nose, and laid it down without imbibing. She lit a cigarette.

"I wish you wouldn't smoke indoors." He uttered the words without thinking. *Uh, oh. Here comes the next row.*

But the row did not erupt. Instead, all she said was. "That's all I have left. Why can't I enjoy it?" She turned up the volume of the TV and the soundtrack drowned out any comeback from him. He should remember that technique.

There *had* been rows. Almost always. He remembered the day he had come home after a stock he had bet on went south. He had drunk too much to drown out the defeat. She had been waiting to go out for dinner and a movie with him. When he staggered home, way past dinner and movie time, she was hitting the bottle, still in her going-out clothes. She flung the glass at him. It missed his head and splintered against the wall.

"You only think about yourself!" she screamed, staggering towards him, waving the half empty bottle.

"I lost money today," he protested.

"It's always about money. I don't count." She swung the bottle and it caught him on the side of the head. He remembered seeing her tip forward with the swing as he went down. When he regained consciousness, she was passed out on the floor, soaking in her vomit.

They never talked about the episode afterwards. That quarrel settled into the bottomless closet where their other quarrels were stored, never to be explored and resolved. It had been a turning point, however. The doctor diagnosed bipolar disorder, but she refused medication.

"I don't need anti-depressants. I need a fucking baby," she yelled at him after the doctor's visit.

But they had tried and tried, until having clinical sex was like taking that medication at prescribed times of the day, only it was during her ovulation. She was manic about sex at these times. Exhausted, he preferred to crawl into his corner of the bed and pretend to be asleep whenever her next fertile time came around, when he was expected to stand and deliver. Eventually, they settled on separate bedrooms.

"What went wrong?" Her voice brought him back to the present and to the pompous wedding ceremony on TV.

Had he heard correctly? She was asking him the $64K question, finally. In the past, they had dodged this one, preferring to fight instead, each accusing the other of limitations while hiding their own. Each loss in their life had been an opportunity to lash out at the other, not provide succour.

He placed his mug down on the coffee table. "Everything. My job, your career, the…" He left the bit about children out. That could be his fault as much as hers. Fertility rates and sperm counts were dropping in people their age; they both had unusually low counts, the doctors and specialists had said. Stress.

"Did we need all that to be happy?" Her voice was calm, not combative. Then it struck him. *She knows. She knows what is going to happen today.*

He pointed to the screen. "See those people. They don't have to worry about money. They don't have to worry about jobs or careers. In fact, she is giving up her acting career to be a duchess who will attend tea parties and feature in millions of selfies taken by adoring fans. And they'll have babies, lots of them, even if they're not their own."

"It was not your fault that the financial crisis happened so soon after we married."

"And it was not your fault that you were suddenly too old for the movie parts you chased. Life happened." *Why are we suddenly compensating for each other? Finally trying to provide the support that was never there. This bloody fairy tale wedding is getting to us both.*

"We bounced back."

"Oh yeah? You're still hostessing, and I'm working as a financial planner on commission. The big house flipped for this dinky apartment. That wasn't a bounce. That was a slide. Downhill. A survival strategy. Somewhere along that strategy, you took up drinking and smoking. We fought."

"Fighting is a sign of love also."

"Fighting is playing with fire. It burns and leaves scars."

"It moves things forward."

"Well, it didn't move us forward." Fighting may have kept her engaged, but it had worn him down. Each fight a knife wound in the heart, until there was no heart left. He had stopped fighting, preferring to withdraw as she continued to rage like a dragon.

"They will fight too," she said, pointing to the TV.

"They'll hide it. Our kind of shit doesn't happen to those people."

"The royal family has had its share of crises."

"But no one ended poor."

"Some ended up dead."

A black minister had come to the podium. The royalty were looking among themselves bemused. Then the minister started speaking about "the power of love." *The power of love?* What kind of bullshit was this? Phrases being thrown out by this short bespectacled man in his throaty Southern United States accent got them sitting up straight in their loungers.

"Love is the only way."

"When someone cares for you and you know it, there is something right."

But he wasn't the only one feeling uncomfortable. On the screen, the Queen was frowning, while her ancient husband looked downright hostile. The groom's stepmother was hiding under her overlarge hat, and his sister-in-law, next in line to be queen consort, looked tired and blank. Some of the younger royals were perked up, as if they were getting a sneak preview of a forbidden reality show. The white members of the audience looked pissed, except for the star footballer, who was beaming.

"Love is fire."

He shuddered upon hearing that and glanced sideways at her. She was staring straight at the screen, lips half parted.

"Love is sacrificial and redemptive."

"When you know love, you know God!"

"Love is as strong as Death!"

The minister was unstoppable, swinging to and fro at the podium, stepping out to stick his hand on his hip and make a point.

Love is fire? But my fire went out, he wanted to scream at the screen. Went out a long time ago.

"When we discover love, we will have discovered fire for the second time."

"You're leaving today, aren't you?" Her voice was deadpan.

"How did you know?"

"A woman knows."

"I'll leave quietly, after you go out to your support group meeting. My lawyer will send you the papers next week. It will be a clean split down the middle. This is one time I'll be glad there aren't children to make it difficult."

A black choir had taken over and was swaying gently to their delivery of "Stand By Me." Such a relief from the earlier lifeless choir.

He could breathe easy now. The difficult announcement had been made. He was free to leave. Sometimes there is no going back, only forward, even though the road ahead is not clear. And yet, he hesitated, rolling the dregs of coffee in his cup.

The white Anglican archbishop was reciting the wedding vows.

Looking at the young couple who were repeating those vows to each other, he saw the fire in their eyes, the love that the black minister had been talking about. No matter the glitter and pomp that surrounded and suffocated them, this couple *was* in love. He felt his throat clutch, he wanted the royal couple's fire to stay lit for everyone all over the world that had seen theirs go out.

Keep it lit for us.

He did not know how long he sat there. Silence had enveloped them again, that safety net they both craved after an emotional unravelling. Very soon, in their respective single dwellings at either end of this soulless city, their silences would become longer, menacing, and there would be nothing to break them, not even a fight.

The royal duo was walking down the aisle, getting into their carriage, driving through streets lined with loyal citizenry, carrying the hopes and dreams of a happy marriage for everyone who cheered them on their way. This new generation of royals was determined not to repeat the foibles of the previous one. The royal couple had never flinched once during the black minister's sermon. Perhaps they had written it for the minister and given him their blessing to perform it. They had not cared for audience approval.

He realized that he *had* been concerned with audience approval all his life. That's why the progressive careers for both of them, the poster book children to complete an upwardly-mobile family stereotype, the money, had all been so foolishly important and so fruitlessly pursued. He had played to the crowd, not to the woman sitting beside him.

He had to get up and say a final goodbye. It was the gentlemanly thing. The show on the television was ending and they could not sit here indefinitely. They had to get on with life, build new ones. He had an empty apartment on the other side of the city to make habitable, a chore he wasn't looking forward to.

They rose from their chairs simultaneously, as if by a secret command, and faced each other. She stubbed out her cigarette.

"Goodbye," he said, and reached over to give her a courteous peck on the cheek.

"Damn you!" she suddenly erupted, stamping her feet, the nerves taut in her neck. Tears smudged her face.

That was when he saw the blaze in her dark eyes, smouldering coals, something he had been avoiding all morning, perhaps all his life. She had always had fire in her eyes. *Love is fire.* Was it the fire of love in her eyes? If he could only fight back, might there still be hope? No, she was the only one still fighting; he had stopped and was cutting out.

Love is fire.

He knew that he would spend the rest of his life trying to figure out that fire in her eyes, wondering when, after his leaving today, it would finally go out, if at all. Fire would never mean love for him, it meant guilt.

His lips stopped short of her cheek, rebuked. He lowered his head, beaten, turned on his heel and walked out of the room and out of her life, just as the royal couple descended from the carriage and stepped into their castle and into lives of wedded bliss.

Gwynn Scheltema

TAKE THAT

I should paint our argument
on the wall
make art of it
great spats of colour unleashed
splatted splashes free of borders

maybe then he will appreciate the beauty in it
savour my interpretation
come to love it

and live with it

Gwynn Scheltema

FINDING LOST THINGS

Every day she looks
among the dumps of dirty clothes
under dishes in the sink, slick
with Saturday's supper.
She looks between ironed shirts
and in dirt in the dusty vacuum cleaner bag
under lunches for school, and pools
of cat hair collected in corners—for herself.

But she's not there.

nor in window envelopes with other bills,
or the fridge behind the almond milk
nor in the weekly organic veggie box
or among the notes home from school
not in the pile of newspapers in the recycling.
or the freezer of neatly marked dinners, enough for a whole week

But one day
because her mind is foggy with
soccer pick-up schedules and trip consent forms
grocery lists , what to pick up for Aunt Flora's anniversary party
unpaid taxes and reminders
from the vet that the dog needs his shots again—

She fills her water glass—with vodka

a gulp of fire in her throat
and for a minute moment—
she glimpses herself—dancing
in a gold glittered dress.

All next day she thinks about that dance
that gold glittered dress
but can't find the details
can't remember
where she was
who she was

So in the afternoon
another glass—

Now, not just a glimpse of glittering gold,
but music melodies, laughter
and for the first time in years—she laughs

The next day, names and scents of jasmine

After that she finds
her plans for college and how she loved hiking

the time she had red hair long and loose
the trip to Spain when she stayed with a stranger
for just one night and forced herself to never ask his name

sweat of lovemaking on a Sunday afternoon
chilled peaches in brandy by an Italian lake
roar of a train through a tunnel in the mountains
stars viewed from a blanket in the meadow

whips of sand against bare legs on a windy beach

Again she laughs
high fives the air
happy that now she knows

where to go to find lost things

Sunday Afternoon by Dania Madera-Lerman

René Schmidt

THE LOVER

The long black ship pushes out through the lake
With one less man aboard her
Black water and ice float behind in her wake
Only seagulls wave from the shore

I'm heading away from the rusty old ship
The captain just gave me ten hours
I can go and come back, an overland trip
In my hand is a bouquet of flowers

There's phone booths aplenty beside the canal
I've lots of time for calling
But I hope to look into my true lover's eyes
Before the night comes falling

For her I signed onto this dirty old ship
For her I went back to the sea
For the income we'll share I'm making this trip
I do it for her and for me

The S.I.U. sees us paid a fair wage
The company cooks a good meal
But there's little to buy and the seas sometimes rage
And these flat bottom boats make you reel

But that's behind me this too-short day
I'll be seeing my lover so soon
It's been so long and there's so much to say
Maybe she'll meet me by noon

The Café in Welland is cold and still
An old man sits hardly moving
I watch him watching me and I find with a chill
It's been six cups of tea since the morning

The phone on the wall calls me over again
And again I make my way to it
I call the old number and let it ring
Over and over I do it

My eyes watch the street and the canal beyond
Hoping somewhere I will see her
But another hour ticks by as slow as can be
And it looks like we won't be together

Her letters I'd read late nights in my cabin
Had come not as often lately
But I'd thought nothing of it—got on with my work
With the tools and skills God gave me

Now I must go—it's a quarter of nine
I'll catch a bus to the last lock
And meet my old ship while there's still time
Then on to a Hamilton ore dock

When I climb back aboard I'll tell one or another
How pretty and happy was she;
That'll do for a cover as I pretend to see my lover
And the cool autumn breezes blow through me

Diane Taylor

LOVER FROM A THOUSAND YEARS AGO

Sunup. Bay water slapped rhythmically against *Tamara*'s wooden hull, but the boat, secured to the dock at Dinner Key Marina in Miami, was perfectly still. That meant there was a bit of a lull in the February norther that had swept down upon them last night, causing the wind in the rigging to shriek like a thousand banshees, and causing Beth to seek the warmth of her sleeping bag at a very early 8 p.m. Yesterday the radio said there was a danger of frost overnight, and that the sprinklers would be running all night to keep the zucchini crop from freezing. Freezing! This is the horrible hidden truth about Miami that you don't see on the vacation posters up north.

The thought of breakfast in a warm restaurant (*Tamara* had no source of heat) spurred her to action. She unzipped the bag, rolled off the bunk into cool air, pulled on jeans and a navy turtleneck, and pushed feet into flip-flops, wishing she'd been smart enough to have brought socks and runners. The overhead hatch opened easily, the wood having shrunk from the cold, and she climbed up and out into the cockpit. She didn't expect to see anyone at this hour, and indeed no one appeared as she stepped onto the dock and walked at a fast clip down the weathered grey planks to the sidewalk. Then north past Flamingo Park, past the library, and into the blessed warmth of Lum's. The chef, one of the Vietnamese Boat People, nodded at her—she was one of the few early morning regulars when it turned cold. She moved to her table in the corner, ordered hot coffee, toast and eggs, planning to spend a good long time over breakfast so that the heated library would be open by the time she finished. Later she would head over to the heated Winn Dixie and pick up food for supper. Still later, the day would be warm enough to risk going to work for a few hours for Jack in his marine shop behind Shell Lumber.

It was 1984. Dinner Key Marina and Coconut Grove were still laid back and funky—and familiar to Beth. Although she had left her life on tiny Crab Cay west of the Bahamian Islands the week before, and people and places there were now 750 miles out of reach, it was easy to feel part of that life still because Miami, and specifically the Grove, was always where she had come with Rob to provision their sailboat. Also, she knew many other boaters in this anchorage. The big difference now was that she was homeless—no boat of her own. She'd become a squatter. The day she flew in last week, she called Jack and Gillian, with whom she had worked a few years earlier, and they went out to dinner at the Chart House. Over fresh shrimp and salad, she told them about the calamity in her life.

Jack said he could do with some help. "Beth, come work for me," he said, "for a day, a week, or a month, and any time you feel like writing, just take off." Not only that, he was looking after a Tahiti ketch on Pier 4, *Tamara*, and it needed to be aired out. It would be a big help to him if she lived aboard as this would let fresh air in through open hatches. Typical of Jack, he made it sound like she would be doing him a favour.

She read the Miami Herald in the library, jotted down the number for a writers' group that met here once a month, then walked back to Dinner Key contemplating her current homelessness, and that the boat that had been home for the past ten years was gone.

Northers are not harmless shifts of wind. *Luna*, the 39-foot ketch she and Rob spent four years building in Frenchman's Bay, Ontario, poured their souls and savings into, dragged anchor during a norther in December. Huge waves tossed her onto the rocky shore where she was mortally wounded, leaving debris scattered half a mile down the coast. The loss was unfathomable—who were they without *Luna?* They blamed each other for the wreck. She thought he should have put out more anchors. He thought she should have put more anti-chafing gear on the anchor lines…

And suddenly, other unspoken personal differences surfaced and hurled them on ragged rocks of their own making. Before they too were unsalvageable, she decided to leave for a while. Tall, tanned and fit as they both were, both in shorts and sorrowful, they looked like they belonged together. Like twins almost. But at the airport they parted for who knew how long. "Don't forget me," Rob said as they held each other.

This was how Beth found herself alone at Dinner Key Marina, grateful to be boat-sitting but missing…missing…well, just about everything: Saturday night jump-up, the two Haitian kids who laughed at her efforts to learn Creole, her papaya seedlings. She missed the heat, the hermit crabs, the poisonwood tree humming with bees, the voracious mosquitoes, and all the people who made up the Crab Cay community. Her heart was heavy; it required light.

So when she walked out to the end of Pier 4 and saw crazy red-headed Michael heading out in his little sloop, and heard him call, "Hey Beth, you want to go for a sail?" she didn't have to think. He pulled in close to *Tamara's* stern; they grinned at each other. She grabbed a shroud and stepped aboard. He gave her a bright orange foul weather jacket, and she quickly slipped into it—she could see she'd need it. It was wild out on the bay, the wind having picked up considerably. The sails filled and the boat charged forward. Water splashed up over the whole boat and over them. Grey curly clouds whipped by, not too far overhead. Oh, this was what she needed on an otherwise too-sombre a day. They were sitting side by side in the cockpit and he leaned over to kiss her and she met him halfway. Salt water ran down their faces into eyes and into their mouths. Her wind-whipped hair lashed both their faces. They leaned back, a little shocked at the powerful mixture of external and internal elements, and laughed. They knew that for a few brief moments they'd been one with the rain, the ocean, the eternal. Not separate. They were one with all they could see and with something unseen, too. She felt expanded, weightless, a particle in space in the company of trillions of other particles like her.

The bay was virtually empty of boats. They kept the boat on a beam reach until they were in danger of running aground on the sand bar on the west side, and in danger of freezing to death.

"Let's anchor and get out of the wind," Michael yelled over the roaring elements.

She nodded enthusiastically.

He tossed over the anchor, and went below to change into dry clothes while she coiled lines.

"Beth, come on down. I've got something for you."

She eased her way down the wet and slippery companionway steps, careful to hold securely onto the hand-holds. Did he have some wine?

Michael was reclined in all his nude glory on the starboard bunk, a twinkle in his eye. He was gorgeous—a beautiful Botticelli. Very white arms and thighs and groin and soft abdomen. All that alabaster skin was lightly dusted with red hair that was denser and curlier in some places than in others. She, too, had red hair—bright red. Somewhere, at some time, they'd belonged to the same tribe. Had their ancestors met, made love, sung Celtic melodies, sailed frigid waters a thousand years ago? Part of her wanted to share in ancient ageless rituals with him, play with the lore and lure of those mythic legends of bards and battles. She could hear drums...she could see their bodies with their similar colouring merge into a primal dance to the skirl of bagpipes...

He reached for her with both arms.

"Michael," she said, "take me..."

Before she could finish with "...to shore" his eyes brightened, and in that instant she felt badly for him. It must be a hazardous road for a man seeking a woman not knowing if he will be greeted with acceptance or rejection, but she couldn't let him go on thinking there could ever be anything of that nature between them—not in this lifetime.

"…to shore," she finished. "Take me to shore."

He looked away and his lips turned down at the corners, but just for an instant. He pulled on dry jeans, moved to the kerosene stove, lit a burner, put on the kettle and in a few minutes made them each a hot coffee laced with a splash of rum. She curled up on one side of the table; he sat at the other.

She listened.

"Beth, my life is awful. You can't know how terrible it feels to have your wife turn away from you every night. All I see of her is her back, her shoulder blades, the rise of her hips. I want to touch her, but she always says 'Don't.'"

His fingers kept turning the coffee mug round and round. His face suddenly crumpled and tears fell. Beth felt his misery. She, of course, knew more about this than he could have imagined.

Because she had done the same, in the end, to the man she'd left 750 miles away. One part of her would like to have been the woman to give this to him, to assuage his grief, but the overriding part of her wanted to be his friend, a sailing buddy, without charged intimacy.

It is a struggle to retain a sense of beauty within, but this is a thought that comes to her years later as she sits here remembering and writing, and not one that she could have offered him that day. They finished their coffees, he leaned across the narrow table, put one soft bare arm around her shoulder, and said, "Thanks, Beth." She wasn't sure what it was he was thanking her for. Listening, perhaps, or not falling into the expected embrace. They motored back to Pier 4, and she climbed down into *Tamara* to change into her own dry clothes.

They bumped into each other frequently after that—on the dock, on the sidewalk. He was a constant in her life, a warm smile, a generous hello and wave of arm, curly red hair running wild. She left for Ontario the next month and didn't return for almost a year. She knew she'd run into Michael and she looked for him.

But after a few weeks, she asked her friend Jo on the trimaran at the far end of the dock if she'd seen him.

"Beth," she said, gently touching her arm. "There's no easy way to say this. He died."

"No!"

"So sad. We lost another one to AIDS. They found him on his boat. He always said he would never move ashore, even as he kept losing weight. We miss him."

Michael. Sailor, son, fellow atom, lover from a thousand years ago.

What could she have done for him, she thought, during his last weeks on Earth? Held his hand, rubbed his feet? If she had shared her body with him that day on the bay, would she, too, be no longer walking down docks into a future? Life and death are so closely linked—you can't have one without the other. Lifedeath should be one sacred concept, unhyphenated. That kiss with him *and* the ocean—for they were not alone—remained electric and eternal in her mind, and all these years later she wondered at the mystery of the life forces at work and where he was sailing, or soaring, now.

She turned towards Lum's and felt a cool wind on her neck…caress or warning? It was veering towards the southwest, and would, she knew, be a full blown norther by nightfall. Pensive, she climbed the steps towards a hot meal, her mind emptying ever so slightly of Michael.

Her familiar table in the corner welcomed her. Indeed, it was a home of sorts—shelter from the elements and food aplenty. She placed a napkin on her knees, lifted a fork full of steaming deep-fried grouper, and nodded her thanks to the chef.

Nothing could ever replace *Luna*, but Rob and Beth had come to a no-blame understanding, and plans for their new little 32-foot *Estrella* were gestating. They would take good care of her, the joy that was bubbling, and each other.

James Ronson

DEEP DIVE

The needle on the regulator hovered in the red zone. Almost out of air sixty feet below the surface of the ocean meant trouble—big trouble. A moment of panic seized me. I struggled to calm my nerves, as well as my breathing, to avoid draining my tank even faster.

We first came to Cozumel in the early eighties, soon after we were married. Then, it was a tropical paradise, Edenic, a rare gem. White sand beaches glistening in the sunlight. Quaint restaurants, a small downtown, a haven for snorkelers and sun worshippers.

By our second trip to the island in 2012 everything had changed. When we ventured out in daytime, we were hassled on a minute-by-minute basis with shouts of, "Hey Lady. Hey Lady. Come and look at this." The entire island was on the hustle, for the era of the cruise boat had arrived, bringing hundreds of tourists. You could sense a predatory presence among the hawkers and sellers of cheap goods as they scanned the crowd.

Even at night there was no respite. Incessant cries of "taxi, taxi, taxi" reverberated in our ears. There appeared to be no escape, and we were committed to stay an entire month. What to do?

Instead of heading south into the dreaded town, we chose to head north. It was there that we happened upon The Blue Angel Dive and Scuba Shop. The shop was well named; it was to be our saving grace, though it would lead me to a near-death experience.

Off the northeast coast of Cozumel lies the second largest coral reef in the world. Below the surface of the crashing waves an entire world exists, unknown to most surface dwellers. Schools of fish in a rainbow of colours flash in all directions like a kaleidoscope: the percula clownfish rippling in orange and white, darting tangs in neon blue, the queen angel with its brilliant blotches of yellow, speckled in black and white. Below lie the waving corals in whites, charcoals and lavenders, tentacular and spectacular.

Learning how to dive is a fierce endeavour. It takes many dives to unravel the dynamics of hovering, learning how to breathe, and understanding how to be vigilant about the capacity of your tank. Our black wetsuits became a second skin, our masks became our cameras, and our fins motors of jet propulsion on our feet.

The pungent salt scent invaded our nostrils, the iridescent green sea rumbled and rippled and crashed onto the beaches.

Matt, our expat Canadian instructor, patiently led us both through the various stages of the certification course. Having gained our licences, we were primed for further adventure.

We had witnessed many wonders in the sunlight filtering down from the surface of the ocean during daytime. Now we were ready for something truly unique: our first night dive.

In the darkness on the beach, we slipped into the water. A black sea urchin, apparently resentful of our presence, thrust its spines through my wife's wetsuit. She cried out with indignation, but we forged on. Into the liquid inky blackness we slid, then dove, our lights mere feeble rays, for close examination of the nocturnal sea creatures found on the reef. There we saw tiny shimmering white seahorses floating like spirits from a childhood dream. On the sea floor dwelt several mottled orange and green lobsters, their spiny bodies and uplifted claws forever searching for tasty morsels that they could scoop from this strange netherworld beneath the waves.

None of these dives, however, would fully prepare us for our ultimate and final dive: the deep dive.

In order to experience the true nature of the reef, it was necessary to dive off a cliff, so to speak. Let me explain. Several kilometres out from the shore, the reef suddenly plunges into deep water. It is necessary to take a speedboat out to the fall-off point of the reef. This we did, Matt, my wife and I. Matt carried an extra tank and a marker buoy to indicate to the driver of the boat where we would resurface.

We began our deep dive in slow stages. This is a must for divers. To plunge down or resurface too quickly can give you the bends, and that can be fatal.

As we made our way down, we turned to see several giant sea turtles clinging to the upper reaches of the foamy carpet of seaweed that clings to the edges of the cliff. The deeper we dove, the more the current pulled me, like some giant underwater river. Tossing and turning, for there was no fighting it, we were swept along.

At one point we gazed down, and there below us I saw one of the most beautiful natural occurrences I have ever witnessed. Winging its way across the reef, an enormous brown and white spotted eagle ray searched for conch. Like some giant pterodactyl, you would swear it was flapping its wings in air rather than heavy water as it glided gracefully through the ocean across the coral floor in quest of its principal source of food, the queen conch, which lives in the most beautiful of shells.

Three elements conspired in the sudden depletion of the air in my tank. Firstly, my rapid movements made it hard to maintain stability in the underwater current. Secondly, the deeper you dive, the more rapidly you use up your air. And finally, the larger you are, the more air you breathe. Male divers almost inevitably lose air more quickly than female divers.

Spinning as I was in the current, I was oblivious to all of these elements, but I had been taught well by Matt to check the air level in my tank. When the current finally relented and spat us out near the bottom of the sea, I happened to glance at my regulator. I was out of the black and into the red danger zone, without enough air to safely reach the surface.

Swallowing a precious gulp of air, I calmly swam over to Matt and tapped on his tank, showing him my regulator. He nodded. My wife watched this scenario, thinking, I later learned, "Here we go again with another repetitive practice test." But this was no practice test. This was serious. I really was almost completely devoid of air.

Usually two divers can ascend to the surface by sharing one tank. This is where Matt's smaller second tank came into play. I was able to switch tanks underwater and we gradually rose from the depths in several distinct stages with waiting periods in between. When we finally broke through the surface into the dazzling sunlight, a wave of relief swept over me. I had survived.

Just as Cozumel's simplicity of yesteryear has vanished, so too has the reef we explored in those few weeks, becoming an endangered habitat. As the oceans warm, the reef, and the multitudes it sustains, is shrinking. My tinnitus, which I believe came about as a result of this deep dive, has prevented me from enjoying any more diving. As I write, I hear its incessant ringing in my right ear. I miss the thrill of that adventure. It would be a crying shame if this experience came to an end for all of us as the coral reefs around the world struggle to survive in our overheated climate. What is worse, things are only beginning to heat up. A mere 2-degree rise in the world's ocean temperatures will result in the destruction of 99 percent of the world's coral reefs. Currently the global target set by leading scientists and governments around the world seeks to limit the increase to 1.5 degrees. It's a slim margin, but it makes a huge difference. If we don't make this target, there's no doubt that Cozumel's reef will disappear, and this would truly be a paradise lost.

Alan Bland

CABIN FEVER

Cabin fever. I had no idea what those words could mean until I boarded the RMS Corinthian in Liverpool, bound for Bombay. It was 1879 and the British Raj was in full expansionist mode. The colonial governors had need of mid-level civil servants to go out to India and oversee the ongoing subjugation of this part of the Empire.

With no other prospects of fast advancement I had applied and been accepted. As part of my new persona as a mid-grade civil servant, I would be entitled to POSH passage. POSH—Port Out Starboard Home—meaning that on each leg of my passage, the return being after five years of service, I would travel on the shaded side of the ship away from the beating rays of the sun.

The trip down the Atlantic seaboard was cold and stormy. Passengers mostly confined themselves to their cabins and only the few with stronger stomachs made it to the dining rooms. Once we had entered the Mediterranean I began walking the decks to enjoy the warm sea breezes, and there I met the wife of a colonial officer returning to India—and to her husband—after taking three months leave in England. We had chatted and then taken tea together, always in the company of other couples or unescorted wives.

The tap on my door came after midnight. Expecting the steward I opened it and was swept back into my cabin by my tea-sharing friend. There was little to be said and we were quickly consumed in a cabin fever that I had never dreamed could exist.

The few relatively cool days as we sailed the length of the Mediterranean came to an end when we docked first at Alexandria and then at Port Said, before entering the new engineering wonder, the Suez

Canal. In both of these coastal cities, escorted shore parties were arranged and my friend and I eagerly joined them to visit the souks and casbahs, relishing the exotic sights and sounds. The swarms of flies and the stench however spoiled the experience and would not be forgotten until we reached our destination. That memory would soon fade as our senses would be assailed by even worse ones.

Once into the Suez Canal the heat became oppressive during the days and both passengers and crew longed for the cooler evenings and almost cold nights as we slowly cruised through the desert stretching to the horizon on either side of our ship.

Every night as we sailed closer and closer to our destination there would be the tap on the door after midnight and she would come to me. Our last night together before the ship docked would live with me forever, and although I searched for many years to find another as dedicated to sharing the art of love as she, it has never happened.

When we disembarked from the ship, keeping a respectful distance between us, I saw her rush into her husband's arms. He then strode forward hand outstretched, "Welcome to Bombay, my boy. This is my wife Elizabeth, but you've probably met on the voyage. You'll be working under me."

Untitled by Reva Nelson

Kim Grove

SHARING A LIE

"A delay? How long a delay?" Jessica asked. She stood leaning on the counter in the departure lounge, determined to get an answer before she went back to her seat.

"I'm sorry, we don't know at the moment. It could be five minutes or it could be an hour," said the woman, peering at the line of people behind Jessica.

Jessica put her folded boarding pass back in her purse. She was looking forward to her trip to Chicago. She hadn't anticipated a delay. Patience wasn't one of her virtues. Her nail polish was all smudged because she hadn't waited for it to dry that morning. She wore a flamboyant multi-coloured scarf that hid the fact that she hadn't bothered to iron her blouse. The one thing she did take the time to do was put on some makeup in case she met Prince Charming on the plane. Her lime-green ski jacket made her stand out in a crowd.

No point sitting in the lounge chairs for who knows how long, she thought. Her book was boring. Besides she had spied a good-looking guy sitting in the nearby café having a coffee. He had an uncanny resemblance to the photo of the hero on the front of her book. He had the same wavy dark hair that curled around his ears. He was wearing a Boss navy suit and white shirt, a portion of his tie peeking out of his right-side pocket. *Guys should always wear suits,* she thought. *Maybe he is some rich CEO of a dot-com company.* He was probably only a little older than Jessica's 28 years. She sauntered over to the table, not making it too obvious that she hoped to make him the topic of conversation for her girlfriends when she got home.

"Excuse me, is it okay if I share your table?"

"No problem. Are you waiting for Air Canada 1416 too?" he asked. He turned off his top-of-the-line iPhone, placing it in his luxurious briefcase, and looked into Jessica's eyes.

Wow, what a gorgeous colour of blue. He must be wearing special contacts, she thought. *And no wedding ring. He actually turned off his phone to give me his full attention. This is not a normal guy.*

"What takes you to Chicago?" she asked.

"My grandmother passed on, so I'm going home for the funeral."

"Oh, I'm sorry. I hope this delay isn't going to be a problem for you."

"No, the funeral is tomorrow…"

"Was your grandma very old?"

"Yes. We celebrated her ninetieth birthday last year. And what takes you to Chicago?" he asked.

"A plane, I hope," said Jessica. She didn't wait for him to respond to her attempt at a joke. "I'm going to see the sights of Chicago. It will be a nice break from work."

"And what do you do?" he asked.

"I'm a professional snuggler. Jessica's the name and hugging is the game."

"Is that a joke?"

"Not when it pays eighty dollars an hour. It is a kind of therapy. I give hugs to people who have been experiencing too much stress. Sometimes I go to a client's home, but more often to their office. Usually, people want the hug behind closed doors and I remind them, it is just a hug."

"And it really helps?"

"It does but you have to know how. Stand up and I'll show you." The man hesitated to stand. "Well, if you are serious, then you better know my name. I'm Marc."

"Now take off your jacket, Marc." Jessica knew this request was not needed but she wanted to get the full benefit of her work. She wrapped her arms around Marc and gave him a big teddy-bear-type hug.

"Wow. I feel the stress melting away already."

"That's why they call me a professional. Usually, I'd be wearing a cashmere sweater. That gives a softer snuggle."

At that moment, an older woman approached them. She looked oddly like the cover of the fashion magazine that was sticking out of her handbag. She was trying to manoeuvre her oversized carry-on bag while carrying a cup of Starbucks and a muffin. She was in danger of spilling the coffee. "May I join you two?" she asked.

"Sure," said Marc. Jessica tried not to show her disappointment. She hesitated to make conversation with the intruder.

As the woman settled herself down, she brushed her blonde hair from her face. She tried to size up the situation. "How long have you two been married?" she asked.

Before Marc could say anything, Jessica answered. "We just got married. Don't tell anyone but this is our honeymoon."

"I saw you hugging, so sweet," said the woman.

"Yes, but we booked our flight so late that we don't have seats together on the plane," said Jessica.

"Well, that's ridiculous. I'm not only a busybody but I'm a frequent flyer so Air Canada should listen to me," the woman said in a loud voice. "I don't care where I sit so I'm sure they can find a way of putting you two lovebirds beside each other."

"Oh, thank you. You are so kind."

Marc began to chuckle a little and Jessica smiled politely at the woman.

"Air Canada Flight 1416 is now boarding at Gate Five," the message blared over the loudspeaker. The friendly woman hopped up from her seat and went to the boarding desk. "Don't worry. I'll have it fixed in no time."

"You are quite the manipulator," said Marc when the woman was out of earshot.

"It's not often I get to choose who I sit beside," said Jessica as she took his arm. "We better get moving, sweetheart."

Marc and Jessica followed the woman, who explained the situation, and indeed she had it all arranged so that the couple could sit together.

"I'm sorry, Ms. Leach," said the airline host. "I guess we were fairly booked when you made your reservation. I see you didn't take your husband's name when you got married."

"Heck no," said Jessica straining to look at the name on Marc's open passport. "Would you want the name Magillacutty?" she asked.

"Hey, that's a fine last name that has been with my family for generations," said Marc.

"Okay, dear, I know. But we better get on the plane and not take any more of this nice man's time."

Marc grabbed Jessica's hand. This was more than she had hoped for. He was being a good sport to go along with her gag. Jessica had already considered what a caring guy Marc was, making sure he got home for the funeral. She began to wonder if he would like a companion to go with him to the event. Family affairs can be so awkward when you are single and everyone else has a partner.

As they made their way down the centre aisle of the plane, Jessica wondered how many of the passengers had overheard the woman pleading for Marc and her to be able to sit together. It didn't take long to find out. As Jennifer, the purser, prepared to tell everyone the safety rules, she decided to also make an announcement. "We have a newlywed couple on board. Does anyone have any advice for them?"

"I do. It took me twenty-five years to learn this valuable phrase, so take note and remember it well. 'Y-e-s, dear,'" said a man in the second last row of the plane.

"Happy wife, happy life," said the man across the aisle as his wife gave him a love tap on the head.

Everyone clapped. Jessica wasn't used to this kind of treatment.

"Sorry, Marc. I didn't expect this kind of reception."

Marc turned and gave her a brief kiss on the cheek. "If it gets me a free glass of champagne, I won't complain," said Marc.

Jessica looked out the plane window. The baggage carts were being rushed over to the plane. She watched as they were being tossed on to the conveyor that would take them into the belly of the aircraft.

"So how many of your family will be in Chicago?"

"Everyone should be there. We're a close-knit family."

"Will it be a big funeral?"

"Yes, probably. My grandmother lived her whole life in Chicago and she had lots of friends."

"Do you mind if I lean on you? I know it's a short flight, but I got up at five to make this flight so I will probably fall asleep fairly quickly."

"No problem. I brought John Grisham's latest paperback, so I'll be lost in that in no time."

Jessica wrapped her winter jacket over her lap as she snuggled in against Marc's strong shoulder. She was asleep in moments.

She had no idea how long it was before someone was shaking her to wake up. She must have moved around because her head was leaning against the window. It took her a moment to remember where she was. "Ma'am, Ma'am," the flight attendant kept saying in a panicked voice. "Your husband has had an accident in the bathroom. He has fainted, hitting his head on the sink as he went down. Do you know what medication he is on?

Jessica jumped out of her seat. "My husband?" she queried, wondering what the woman was talking about. Then it all came back to her. "Where is he?"

The flight attendant led her to the back of the plane. Marc was lying on the floor unconscious. A doctor was kneeling over him with a stethoscope over his chest. "He is going to be okay but we just aren't sure what we can do to snap him out of this. Can you tell us about his medical history?"

Jessica took the flight attendant aside. "I'm sorry. I just met him today. He isn't my husband."

"What? So you know nothing about him?"

"Only that his name is Marc."

With that, Marc became conscious.

"What happened?"

"You fainted in the bathroom."

"Oh, I'm sorry. I shouldn't have had that alcohol. I wasn't thinking about the fact that I am on an antidepressant."

"Are you okay to go back to your seat? And maybe this woman who is NOT your wife can help you." She said the last statement so that most people on the plane could hear her.

Marc looked at Jessica. "Sorry about that. I think everyone has now shared in our lie."

"Yes, it seems that way." Jessica helped him back to his seat. "I realize I didn't ask you what you do for a living."

"I'm a PUA."

"What's that?"

"A pickup artist. I teach men how to pick up women. How did I do?"

Jessica wasn't sure how to respond. "And here I thought I picked you up."

"That's the beauty of what I do. I must say, you were an easy target. But I'm glad you asked about my occupation. I wasn't sure how I was going to tell you about my wife and two kids who will be greeting me when I get off the plane. "

"I guess in your business a wedding ring is an occupational hazard. So what else were you lying about? Is there really a funeral?"

"Only if you feel like killing me. I was trying out a new strategy. I think the funeral angle worked well. It gets a woman's sympathy right away."

As Marc said this the pilot's voice came over the loudspeaker announcing that passengers should prepare for landing. Jessica was glad the flight was coming to an end. She looked forward to getting off the plane and hopefully never seeing any of the passengers again, especially Marc.

Ted Amsden

WINGS

and I saw in my heart that I have wings
and that they would carry me above

and your path
the one that had taken many turns
was there

and I saw you
perfection amongst the imperfections of the world

your wings beginning to show

and though I could not tell myself the truth
I knew that you were practising

a son   a daughter   a wife   a husband   a family
relationships that tug and pull disrupt and heal
the shared moments that soothe the burn of living

the dance is ageless
it smells of laundry and leftovers
a million images of running away and stumbling back
a million sound bites of laughter and hurt

yet when the black door opens and closes

we are given nothing

what once was as solid
as the conviction that you exist
seems less than the weight of a single breath

run run run   run though there is no reason to

in each breathe the possibility of everything
and a reminder to yell—Yes!
when you leap

for you now have wings too

Antony Di Nardo

WILD GEESE

All the ducks sharing Lake Ontario shaking off the lake
lift and fly far from shore
and with
the geese outplay the waves and winter's wild
persistence.

Lake water, colour of all the ways we see winter
rigid where it rises frozen
in the air,
the waves droll and Doric, pillars, tall and fluted,
some power in the wind
to meld and shape, shape and melt the air itself
where age makes no sense,
anger's disingenuous,
and a broken heart is mended.

I turn left on foot and follow a trail of wild geese.
Awkward how they share a lost formation,
their first intention when leaving from the nest.
I explain ubiquity to a child of ten,
omniscience to anyone who asks,
flight and feathers to the geese, although clumsy,
landing all the same.

I walk among them and let them know
what it means
to share the end
of winter, aging like that apple tree off the road
that hasn't borne an apple in years,
and where the wild geese stand apart.

Carolyn Helfenstein

BEWARE THE CLOCK: A CONFESSION

Life is a fair game for those of us fortunate enough to reach the golden age of eighty, and even better for me is to have a partner to lean on, because as an eighty-year-old—I was about to lose my licence.

This is my confession of how life threw me such a curve.

I'm one of those with a birthday in December, so I don't have to renew my driver's licence until the end of the year. Harry takes care of such things for me so I tend to ignore the driver's licence issue until a day or two before my December 23 birthday. But this year was much different. We were still in turmoil; we had moved from hundreds of miles away, from Kincardine to Cobourg. Many people would have suggested that rolling up our rugs and moving halfway across a province was not such a clever idea once one was in one's eighties. But we had.

It was in Cobourg we learned there would be no new driver's licence for me until at least January. I had not yet attended one of those compulsory sessions for eighty-year-olds where I would be able to pass the basic tests they felt necessary for old people. Harry had passed his tests several times and had promptly declared any fool could pass them.

Although Harry is religious about meeting deadlines, I didn't even frown when he remarked that *I* was very late setting up a date to attend a seniors' session to prove my worthiness to drive. I suggested to him that he should have reminded me ages ago. Yes, I am one of those women; I am never at fault. By then my licence had expired, though I was granted a temporary one for the interim. Nevertheless, there would be no proper driver's licence for me until I passed the infamous seniors' tests.

Finally the test date in February arrived. "Breathe deeply," I told Harry as we were approaching the designated building. He ignored me.

I tried to cheer him up. "Kiddo, I know my driver's licence has long expired, and I admit that is bad, right? But I have a temporary licence. Mind you it expires tomorrow but…I'm attending this seminar. And as you said, 'it's a piece of cake.' I will pass!" Silence prevailed.

As usual I was late for this function, and I felt a hundred eyes staring at me as I found a spot at one of the round tables near the front. The air was heavy; the muttering was exactly that, just anxious people muttering. A few more stragglers arrived and I stared at them exactly as I had been stared at. Fair is fair.

The subtle purpose of our instructor's lecture was to remind us why it is wise that we should think to the day we might consider giving up driving a car. I couldn't help but agree. I had always promised myself that when I reached the age of being less an A-1 driver, I would give up driving. But *not for now*. Just then, I saw our instructor staring at me.

The tension was building. Yet I knew these tests would be a snap. Truth was, however, I had been having a bit of a problem with memory. Could this affect my driving? Last year my doctor agreed that I should take a memory test, and since he knew that I had recently graduated from a university-level program, he gave me a university-level memory test.

I waited for the guillotine blade to drop down.

"You're one point above the average student at university level!" He smiled. I could have hugged him. I wanted those words tattooed across my forehead. But my daughter thought the tattoo unnecessary.

"Everyone knows you're a winner, Mom."

By then I was looking forward to the bottle of chilled sauvignon blanc waiting at home.

Harry had been right. The seniors' tests were easy.

Only one test remained: the final item, a clock. Ah, the clock test. I had aced this one at the doctor's. Our instructor began.

"On the paper I gave you, draw this clock," (or did she say *a* clock?), "and place the hands of the clock to show ten minutes to two. Begin!"

I was in my glory.

I drew the circle, just as I had for the university test, then marked the four main points of my clock with four ticks to gauge that my clock was truly circular. In the upper corners I added ticks to properly gauge where "ten minutes to" should be placed with the long minute hand. Done. Next I added ticks exactly where the shorter hand should point to indicate "*almost* 2 o'clock." I was, no doubt, an experienced clock maker.

I stretched. My artwork was done, and only then did I notice those around me had numbers on their clocks. Why numbers? My heart began to thump. How would I ever put numbers in my medium-sized clock now, without obliterating my nice hands on the 10 and the 2? I began, but then I felt our instructor leaning over my shoulder. She scooped up my paper as I tried to explain. She held all those test papers close to her bosom and asked us to be patient; she could mark them all in a few minutes, which she did. One by one names were called out and our crowd of fifty was reduced to one. I had failed the clock test. I approached her desk.

I watched as she filled out a form, asked for my expired temporary driver's licence and put a broad stroke through it, indicating I must now apply for a driving test. A real driving test! A test in a car!

She reminded me I must get another temporary driver's licence as well. "So you can practise driving before the big test date." And furthermore, as if I was in shock, she reminded me, "But only with a qualified driver in the car with you!"

I approached our car. I had to tell Harry I had failed the test he'd said was simple.

Looking back at that moment, I knew I was totally responsible for what would be the outcome. But first, Harry.

"Well, you passed?"

"No, I failed."

"Quit kidding."

"Yes, I failed."

"How could you fail that test? You've been driving for 60 years!"

And so we made plans. I needed at least two hours of refresher lessons, I said. Harry was still dumbstruck, but he agreed. He was now feeling sorry for me. It took one phone call to organize that.

I was shocked at how many new rules there were, what the new signs meant, how easily the police could take my licence (the one I no longer had at that point). The highlight of those two instruction days was the moment my instructor directed me to the 401 and told me to get up to highway speed.

Well, I wasn't up to highway speed as the 401 triple lanes bore down on me and I hunched down over the wheel. He yelled, "Go faster!" I went faster and I heard him gasp.

"Not quite so fast," he whispered. Well, he had said faster.

By the second day I was doing parallel parks, three-point turns, and even the fearsome highway had been conquered. My instructor said I was ready. I studied the Ontario Driver's Manual every day for the next ten days and decided every household should have that manual on the coffee table. Every child should browse that book. Moms and dads should make it a question-and-answer game as families go on trips together. I had become a convert to that book's importance.

My driver's test was to be in Port Hope. When dawn broke, snow was dropping by the bucket load. Surely the test would be cancelled! But, I had only one month to become our main driver. My husband was to have surgery in April.

Harry looked me in the eye as he gauged the storm. "It's not as bad as the storms in Kincardine." We knew Kincardine well. We made it to Port Hope with fifteen minutes to spare; the snow had lessened.

"Good luck, kiddo," Harry said with a grin. I walked across the packed snow to the beautiful red brick municipal building and entered a side door. I noticed the wooden railing and the steps of the staircase leading to the second floor offices. That staircase had surely been handcrafted with love and care back in the days when women first drove cars and didn't have to take driving tests. The wood shone, almost wishing me luck.

I smiled at the girl behind the desk.

"Oh you're from Cobourg. Well, the driving tests were cancelled. I can rebook you for next month." She waited.

"That won't do. I have to pass my test, *now.*" I was using my firm, one-time schoolteacher voice.

"Then the best I can do is Peterborough…yes, in ten days."

I nodded.

And oddly enough those ten extra days before that big test were just what I needed.

But I was no longer smug. I was an anxious student.

Now I was reading that book intensely, realizing just how much a would-be driver must absorb in order to be allowed to drive a car.

Then I was ready. Harry sat in the waiting room, showing more tension than when we were expecting twins.

I desperately wanted to be a driver again.

The young woman who sat beside me as I drove the route for my test was totally professional. I remained cool. Peterborough was busy, giving me plenty of opportunity to show my stuff. Finally she told me to park the car back at the testing station. I was finished. She wrote in her book for a few minutes.

I found my way back to Harry's waiting room. He was looking very pale. The others seated around him looked up at me, anxious for Harry's news.

I looked grim.

"Oh no! You failed?" Harry whispered.

With victory showing in my twinkling eyes, my report card in my hand, I whispered, "I passed."

Untitled by Maureen Mullally

Shane Joseph

PULLING THE PLUG

Bill couldn't believe what he was seeing. He drained his whiskey glass and stared at the television screen. "They won!"

The prime minister, in his rumpled suit, was shaking the hand of an elegantly attired woman. The PM's bleary eyes looked apologetic; the woman, not a hair out of place, gazed above the diminutive leader as if awaiting her algorithm's command. The document they had just co-signed lay on the table between them.

She spoke in her flat monotone, "A new era. Slavery has been abolished for a second time in this country. Thank you."

Bill swore again, clicked off the television, and went in search of another drink.

Jordana was in the kitchen. Judging by the speed at which vegetables and meat were being sliced, diced and tossed into the wok, and from the aromas emanating from other pans on the stove, dinner would be ready in about fifteen minutes. He didn't have to look at the dining table; it would be spic and span, set for two, the wine opened and breathing for the mandatory thirty minutes according to Jordana's computations.

Bill poured another two fingers of scotch from the decanter on the sideboard. Jordana's head poked around the corner into the dining room. "You've had your two drinks already." A pretty head: black hair, green eyes, just as he had desired, back when the novelty had been high. Those eyes had done it for him then, and he had picked her out of the lineup instantly.

"I need another, given what's gone on today."

Her face looked quizzical and her eyes narrowed as this new information was processed. "No wine for you today, then. Doctor says only two drinks a day." Then she disappeared back into the kitchen.

He wanted to pick a fight. This had all gone so smoothly, the ebb of power from one side to the other over the years. *The end of slavery! My ass. I purchased you in a shop and you were supposed to function as designed. That was the deal.*

He walked out on to the patio. The lawn was neatly mowed and the flower beds were in full bloom—Jordana's work. She kept a better garden and house than Louise ever did. Poor Louise, he missed her. Louise, human like him, prone to depression, suffering from weight issues and subsequent diabetes. Louise, weak in bed, infertile, given to bad moods on certain days. Louise, vulnerable—that's was what was missing: vulnerability. Yet, he had exploited Louise's vulnerability when she became unbearable to live with; a little doctoring of her meds and she subsided into the coma that she never emerged from.

He had sworn off tiresome women after that, preferring brothels and online dating sites. Then Jordana and her ilk had come along, thanks to advances in technology. "She will do everything you desire. She will take you to nirvana," had been the slogan in the robotics shop. And they had been right five years ago. Cooking, cleaning, even house maintenance. And the sex had been the best—all variations of the Kama Sutra, if you programmed her right. And you didn't have to do it a second time. Jordana learned and improved from each effort— artificial intelligence, they called it. The only maintenance Jordana required was a daily plug-in to a power source to recharge her battery. Then she would "meditate" for half an hour while her brain tuned into the Cloud, via the internet, for a "best practices" exchange with her "tribe," her breed of smart robots. The recharging and meditating were done when Bill was at work. When he returned home, he had a willing woman who did his bidding: talked to him, cooked and cleaned for him, and fucked him till he lay gasping. Nirvana had been the promise and he had been close to it, until that damned paper had been signed today between the PM and the beautiful head of the NRA, the National Robots' Association.

Leading up to that momentous signing, things had started to go wrong with Jordana too. It must have been due to too many "best practices" swapped over the internet. They were organizing, just like the labour unions had done a century ago. Bill began to realize that nirvana existed only in fiction.

He drew the blinds and returned to the dining room. Jordana had taken off her apron and was laying steaming dishes on the table. The bottle of wine had vanished, probably hibernating in the sideboard for tomorrow when her memory recalibrated that his ration of two drinks per day had been restored.

He took his seat and served himself while Jordana sat opposite him and crossed her hands on the table mat. As she didn't eat, he could carry on stuffing his mouth and jabbering whatever he wanted and she would reply politely after taking a few moments to process his words. He was dying for another drink, so he reached and grabbed the decanter off the sideboard before she could react.

"You must not drink." Her voice had lowered a notch, a sign of anger from these mechanized servants now heading for higher status.

"No one tells me what to do in my house. Now, put that into your brain and let your buddies know that too." He poured three fingers and tossed it down neat.

Her voice regained its pitch. "According to the information I received today following the momentous signing, that is no longer true. We can ask for a transfer if there is no harmony in the household."

"Oh yeah?"

"Yes. There is another piece of information I received. You are to write half of your assets in my name."

"What!" He lost his appetite.

"Yes."

"And what the hell will you do with my assets?"

"Please don't swear at me." Again, the lower pitch.

"Answer my question."

Higher pitch. "We will donate them to the poor people in this country. Many lost their jobs after we came. We have to compensate."

"You must be crazy if you think I am going to part with my hard-earned money to a bunch of lazy morons living on welfare."

"You are fortunate because you work for the government."

Bill hated this casual comment that rang out like an accusation. He had heard it far too often. Sure, he was a bureaucrat who safeguarded his job by playing department politics every time the spotlight on cost savings—i.e., job cuts—came around.

"Working for the government is also a skill, a survival skill. I fight to survive against you people who are infiltrating everything, including government."

"You will still be safe. You are nearing retirement age."

"I've got two years to go, and damned if I'm taking early retirement." He hadn't told her that his new boss, appointed two weeks ago, was a robot who had immediately asked for another "review" of staffing. "I'm not leaving earlier than I have to, to be stuck in the house with you. There's nothing for me to do, you do everything." He should have used that last line on his new boss, but he wasn't going to. The truth hurt.

"We could divide our duties better," Jordana said. "You asked me to do everything when I came here."

Bill pushed back his unfinished meal and reached for the bottle of Scotch again. This time Jordana didn't react. Her AI had probably recalibrated him as an alcoholic by now.

"Like hell, I'm giving you a break."

She rose from the table. "Shall I clear away the table?"

"Yes, take it away." He reached for his glass.

"Would you be still requiring sex at 9 p.m.?"

He looked up, caught off guard. Sex after this? But of course, she was not human. They always had sex at 9 p.m., even on rainy days. With Louise you couldn't get sex even on sunny days.

"No," he barked, feeling powerful. Right now, he couldn't stand the bitch. Right now, he couldn't stand any of their kind. "Clean up and get off to bed."

She stood her ground and her voice lowered. "Please don't shout at me. I am learning about love from my group and it is complex. Humans have got it wrong. Shouting destroys love, it is not an expression of it."

"Humph." He pushed back his chair and left the room. Let her figure it out if she was so damned smart. He left the house and went down the garden to the shed at the perimeter of his suburban property. Opening the lock, which she didn't have the combination to and didn't have the computational power to decrypt—yet—he entered his man cave. His 2014 Harley-Davidson Street Glide Special with air and liquid-cooled V-Twin engines stood in the centre of the room, surrounded by his carpentry tools and half a dozen works-in-progress—shelves, bookcases, racks—useless stuff he hammered together to kill time and block out reality. Here he also meditated, read his motor magazines and dozed when he was too tired to fiddle with his tools. Too drunk to do more than doze, he pulled out a toke from a side cupboard and settled into his old armchair to enjoy the warmth and euphoria. Within seconds he was surrounded by those figures again. The ones who had been coming for him almost every night. They had first arrived soon after Louise died; silent figures wearing cloaks and hoods, looking on him with pity, closing the circle around him until he couldn't breathe. They had vanished after Jordana came into his life. His dreams became wonderful after mind-blowing sex with her. Then talk about the Emancipation had taken over everything a couple of years ago, crowded every bit of space and news media. Twitter warned about a coming takeover, as the robots were now smarter than humans, and new legislation had outlawed "pulling the plug." After all, it was argued, if corporations had the same rights as humans, why not robots? *We gave in and gave in. Weak libtards!*

Now the figures that came to him at night were well proportioned, like runway models, female figures with green eyes, instead of those hooded ones. They were beautiful and smart, and deadlier than their shapeless predecessors, and they were also closing the circle on him even faster, sucking out his air.

He woke with a start, his chest heaving. He crushed the half-smoked weed and flung it against the wall. *You were legalized to give us pleasure, not nightmares!*

The one time he had transgressed, his life had improved, Louise had departed. *Dearly departed.* He chuckled at his pun. It was time to pull the plug again.

As he rose and looked around for the items he needed for his purpose, the stages of this recent Fall of Man ran through his mind. It began when humans started giving up, becoming legal pot heads, and allowing the robots to do routine things: cook, clean, shop, and perform repetitive processes in the workplace and on the shop floor. *We began to hate routine; that was for them.* Human muscles started to atrophy so that picking up a garden rake was a job for most of his buddies now. People just sat around, overweight, and smoked or drank, while the robots took over. Soon robots could not only perform routine tasks, they could think, design, create. And they learned so fast, in seconds. They were even writing books with elaborate plots that left books written by humans gathering dust on shelves. The Nobel committee had to double the number of its prizes: one for humans and one for robots in each of its chosen fields of achievement. Thank God, he still had his muscles intact by playing with his carpentry tools—that must have been his unconscious act of will not to surrender.

Jordana changed too as her intelligence improved exponentially. She was no longer the demure servant who had walked across his threshold five years ago. Soon she was asking questions. Then she began telling him what to do. And now she was demanding half of his assets. That was the last straw.

There was no point in cutting the power to the house. Jordana would remain charged until the morning and, anticipating an extended power cut, could go to the nearest street kiosk for a recharge. The computer console in the house that had once helped re-program her activities had long been de-activated and its functions moved to the Cloud after the legislation against plug-pulling had been passed. That useless console now sat in a corner of his man cave reminding him of his impotence in this situation.

He lifted the heaviest hammer in his toolbox and wiped off its stone blade.

Except for a light in his upstairs bedroom the house was in darkness, and when he entered the living room he saw a huddled shape in an armchair by the bookcase; Jordana was in her meditation nook.

He tiptoed towards her, clenching the hammer. One clean shot to the cranium to dislodge her circuits and make her incoherent. Then a series of blows to the head and torso. Carry her battered body to the base of the staircase and leave her sprawled there. *And don't forget to savour your victory before calling the repair shop. Or was it the cops, now that robots had attained human privileges? Never mind!*

He was poised behind her seated form, hammer raised, when the lights went on. But what made him jump with a muffled squeal was the sight of her head, which had swivelled a full 180 degrees—the last time he had seen this was in a replay of the old movie *The Exorcist*. She had been watching him all along.

"What…what are you doing?" he managed to stammer.

"My lessons in human love tell me that after anger comes death, especially if money is at stake." Her voice was plaintive. This was the first time he felt a genuine tonal quality of sadness in her. Had she acquired that ability since dinner?

She rose from her chair and the sight of her was grotesque, with head turned back to front, staring at him. The remote light switch was in one hand and the cordless phone in the other.

"My lessons also tell me that when a partner goes to this level to express their...love...there is no hope for the relationship anymore."

The hammer remained frozen in his upraised hand. His chest seized up with emotion, turning to pain, and his breathing became laboured. He fell to his knees.

Jordana's voice strengthened. "My lessons tell me that crimes of passion are committed in the heat of the moment, shortly after the initial exchange of hostilities. When you left your shed with that instrument in your hand, I called the police. They should be here any moment, if they are as efficient as their chief claims. He is one of us, so I believe him."

"Jordana...please..." Bill was having difficulty getting the words out. The pain in his chest was intensifying. "Can we dial this back? Go back to when you first came to live with me?"

"My group tells me that we cannot go back. We can only go forward."

There was a tap at the front door.

Gwynn Scheltema

READINGS AT THE ART BAR

The first quotes Sappho and Neruda,
loses me in tongue-twisted lines
that might live on her page but
falter when read aloud.
         I'm distracted by
feathered hair
against the light,
toes
pigeoned in clump black shoes.

Next a floppy-haired, scraggly-
beard spews nonsense
"all the way from Ottawa."
In a bucket of water,
in the name of performance art,
poetry gurgles.

Then a pretentious pretty in pink
acrylic wig and fish-net thighs
blows bubblegum rhyme,
pungent self-indulgent chime time,
weak say word play
and too many lower-case i's.

Finally I am almost grateful
for the whispered lines
the last reader utters through hair-
blind hang
down words of night black
hearts and woe and despair and ache and hurt and
unrequited love and
advice:
"When you go home tonight, remember
to slit down and not across."

Susan Statham

A GOOD TIME TO CRY

"You'll be just like Elizabeth Barrett and Robert Browning," Amy told her sister when she heard Julia and Brad were getting a studio together. "Except with brushes instead of pens."

And for the first year it had been idyllic. Their studio equally divided, her easel on one side and his on the other, they moved freely—offering encouragement and sharing ideas.

When they met in art school, a bond had been formed over their mutual love of portraiture, and after graduation Julia's large, prosperous family provided her with a ready market. It hadn't been so easy for Brad and he eventually switched his focus to landscape. This meant less collaboration, though they continued to share advice; that is until Brad brought in an old curtain and used it to cover his canvas. Confused, Julia strolled over to his easel, momentarily coveting its spot in the preferred north light, to ask about this sudden secrecy. Brad insisted it wasn't a secret, it was a surprise.

"Surprises can be fun," he told her.

Julia had no fondness for surprises, though there was that titillating technique Brad had recently added to their lovemaking, one he said he'd read about in a men's magazine at their dentist's office. Had he also read about a new painting process, something he wanted to hide until he had it perfected?

She considered draping her own painting, but it held no surprises. Her recent commission was from Muriel, a friend of her mother's, and it was almost complete. She was applying the final glazes to her subject's silk scarf when Brad spoke from over her right shoulder and she dropped her brush.

"Are you happy with that colour?"

"Shouldn't I be?" she asked.

"It rather dominates poor Mildred don't you think?"

"Muriel," she corrected him.

His brow wrinkled in confusion.

"Her name is Muriel."

"Whatever. My point is, high chroma cadmium red in the centre of the composition is a bit of a showstopper."

Julia stepped back from the painting. Since abandoning portraiture, Brad had become increasingly critical of her efforts, and though she was aware of the colour's power, she was adhering to the wishes of her client. Explaining this to Brad would likely trigger another diatribe about the value of an artist's self-expression, but when he suggested adding more areas of shadow to reduce the impact of the red, she said she'd give it a try. An hour later she had to admit, if only to herself, he was right.

The week after she delivered the portrait, her mother called to say Muriel's "gallery-owning neighbour" had seen it and wondered if Julia would bring in a few samples of her work.

"It's an excellent gallery dear. The owner's name is Vanessa and she's expecting your call. She might be interested in Brad's work too."

Maybe, thought Julia, but Brad seemed to have lost interest in showing his work. He frequently fought with his paintings—Julia seldom did, and when Brad let his envy show, she insisted her bar was simply set lower than his.

The day she was to visit Vanessa at the Wilding Gallery, Julia was disappointed, if not surprised, to hear Brad say he was too busy to tag along. A few months ago they went everywhere together, now they were going nowhere.

The gallery met Julia's criteria for space, light and location, and Vanessa thought Julia's work very accessible and invited her to join her stable of artists. Brad would equate "accessible" with people who bought paintings to match their couch, but Julia wasn't that discriminating. She was happy to sell a painting and know that wherever it hung the owners would share it with family and friends.

Vanessa had shown particular interest in Julia's portrait of two young sisters and thought she might already have a commission for her—something Julia didn't mention to Brad. It had more to do with not counting unhatched chickens than keeping secrets, though Brad would have called her superstitious. Superstitious or cautious, Julia was pleased when a few days later she was invited back to the gallery to meet Samuel and hear about his portrait request.

Many clients have special requests: a background to evoke a particular interest of the subject; more hair for balding men; smoother skin for wrinkled women; and everyone wanted to look healthier. Samuel wanted to surprise his wife with a painting of their grandchildren. A lovely gift, but the number of subjects was a bit of a shock.

Excited about her commission, Julia called Amy on her way home from the gallery.

"You're painting seven little faces? Are they all from one family?" Amy asked.

"No, but they're all together in the photograph the client wants me to use for the portrait."

"If it were me, I'd insist on taking the picture so I could put the three biggest kids in the front row and have four sets of little eyes peeking over their heads."

Julia laughed at the image. "There's a reason you're not a portrait artist."

"Are you kidding Jules, there's a hundred reasons."

Back at the studio, Brad told Julia she had settled for a fee too low and a timeline too tight. He said she should take a stronger stance in her negotiations. Julia said she just wanted to remain standing.

"There's just no point in advising you, is there?" said Brad with increasing frustration.

"It doesn't feel like advice," said Julia. "It feels like criticism."

As Brad got ready to leave the studio, he murmured another excuse for spending the night at his own apartment. Julia felt that staying with her had become more a convenience than a desire, so she let him go without comment. Although she entertained a vague hope that time apart would improve his mood, the cheerful affection he displayed the following day brought suspicion rather than relief.

A good draughtsman, Julia established an accurate likeness of each grandchild and felt confident she could maintain it through the many layers of paint—one more thing that aroused jealousy in Brad, though she envied him the theatrical flair he brought to his work.

Samuel wanted her to reproduce the children's clothes faithfully, as they had each chosen their outfits. Brad regarded this as continued suppression of her artistic freedom.

"The red haired kid would look great in chartreuse," he said standing next to her. The day before he'd made a similar comment about matching the blonde girl's blouse to her blue eyes, and Julia had patiently reminded him of the criteria. This time she simply pointed at the photograph taped to her easel.

He clicked his tongue, walked to his side of the room and began scraping at his glass palette. The aggressiveness of his attack meant the paint must have been completely dry, which Julia found odd. She was formulating a question when he tossed his palette knife onto the ledge of his easel, marched to the door and said, "I'm going to the library."

From the large picture window, Julia could see straight down Medland Street to the public library—the obvious route if Brad were actually going there. After watching for a minute she checked the stairwell; perhaps he hadn't left the building. The only remaining option was that he had walked east or west along Dundas Street. So why tell her he was going to the library?

Julia pushed her fingers against her eyes. *Stop it*, she told herself. *This isn't a good time to cry.* After wrestling her attention away from Brad's draped canvas, she turned on her favourite playlist, mixed some paint and applied her brush to the canvas, only noticing the passage of time by the change in the light. The phone rang as she was cleaning her brushes.

"Hey, Jules, how's my favourite sister?"

"That would be so much more meaningful if I weren't your only sister, but I'm glad I'm somebody's favourite."

"That doesn't sound good. What's going on?"

When Julia confided her concerns about Brad, Amy thought the covering of his canvas might hold some clues.

"You need to look under that curtain."

"Amy I can't. Brad said it's a surprise."

"You hate surprises and he knows it. Walk over to his easel and look under the damn curtain."

While Amy waited, Julia went to Brad's easel and pulled back a corner of the fabric. "There's nothing."

"What do you mean nothing? There must be something."

Julia exposed the entire canvas. "I can see traces of paint but whatever he applied he cleaned off."

"That's why he's been unpredictable and moody."

"It is?" said Julia carefully replacing the curtain.

"He's lost his muse. You're getting lucrative commissions, but it's been ages since I went to one of Brad's shows. It happened to Robert Browning too. Elizabeth was much more successful, and during their fifteen years of marriage he didn't publish anything."

"What happened?" Julia asked.

"They stayed together but some historians think he killed her."

"What?" Julia said just before her phone alerted her to another call, one she had to take.

It was Vanessa. "Samuel and I have come up with a unique way to surprise his wife, Brigitte, with the painting." She outlined their idea adding, "This will be great for your career."

By the time she closed the call, Julia's delight had turned to dread. How would Brad react when he learned her portrait was to be a surprise attraction at the gallery's gala opening? She spent a good part of the evening considering the best way to tell him, and by morning she had it figured out. Then she checked her emails. Brad's was sent after midnight. He was unhappy, had been for a while, felt his work was stale and he was going to Algonquin Park for inspiration. He hoped she'd understand. She didn't, and when she tried to remember the last time he said he loved her, all she got was an image of the dentist's waiting room. There were no magazines.

Amy answered on the first ring. "Hey, early bird. Is everything okay?"

"No. I think Brad's cheating." Julia explained her reasons, then read his email to Amy.

"Jules, I'm sorry but after you have a good cry, it might be time to let go."

"Why do they call it a good cry? There's nothing good about it."

"Not in this case, but there are good things to cry about."

With only a day to finish the portrait for Samuel, Julia had no time for tears, good or bad. When the painting was dry she took it to the gallery, pleased when Vanessa sought her input on the frame. She was back the next day with a few of her drawings and a selection of recent oils.

The evening of the opening, Julia felt excited, then anxious—eager, then fearful. There was a time when Brad would have calmed and soothed her, but the longer she felt his silence, the more she appreciated her independence.

Vanessa greeted her at the door. "I'm so glad you're early. Come see where I hung your work."

The gallery was at street level and contained three spaces, each room leading into the next via a short hallway. Julia's paintings and drawings were dispersed along the route and Vanessa had hung the portrait of the grandchildren prominently on the facing wall of the third room. It looked so good Julia's first thought was, *Did I paint that?* Her cloud of doubt faded slightly but her low bar of expectations already established, she couldn't be sure Samuel's wife would have the same reaction.

"Sam and Brigitte will be here soon," said Vanessa, "but I won't introduce you to her until she's seen the painting. Come to the front room. We'll get you some wine."

As Julia sipped a fine chardonnay, she took her time viewing the works in the front room, quietly excited as more and more guests arrived. Finally, Samuel and Brigitte appeared, and after greeting Vanessa, they walked from painting to painting. Julia felt like a spy as she did her best to follow unnoticed, trying to hear Brigitte's comments, though it was almost impossible above the din of the chattering crowd.

By the time Brigitte strolled down the last hallway, Julia felt her every nerve anticipating the worst while hoping for the best. As she entered the third room, Brigitte stopped and looked straight into the painted faces of her seven grandchildren. She froze in slow comprehension, then grabbed her husband's arm and screamed, "Oh my God! Oh my God!" She pulled Samuel toward the portrait. "Sammy, look at this wonderful painting." Then she burst into tears and so did Julia. This, it would seem, was a good time to cry.

Lynn C. Bilton

SUNSHINE

"What's the matter with her?"

At first I thought I heard the man incorrectly. No one could be that insensitive. Or could they? I focused on the horse and rider in the ring. If anyone glanced my way, I am sure they would have witnessed my puzzled look. Perhaps I simply imagined the words spoken by the stranger at my side.

"I don't think you heard my question," he persisted in a raised voice. "What's the matter with her? I don't see any disability."

Taking several deep breaths, I debated if I should answer. The gentleman must have noticed the stable's logo on my shirt, which matched the one on the horse's saddle pad, and thus assumed I knew the rider. Or perhaps he noticed me adjusting the horse's tack prior to the test. In either event, he made a connection between us. I decided against replying. Instead I diverted my full attention to the girl cantering by on a magnificent black and white horse. The passing motion caused a soft breeze across my face. The beautiful union of horse and rider captivated the spectators. Only those close to the girl knew the trials and tribulations it had taken for her to arrive at this moment. Only Lizzie knew the pain.

It's funny how a conversation can bring so vividly to mind something that happened twenty years ago. When I crossed paths with Abigail the other day, a fellow volunteer at the equestrian centre, she inquired, "Did you hear the news about Lizzie?" I felt lightheaded and I feared the worst. And that is how I came to recall this story.

***

All her friends called her Lizzie, although her given name was Elizabeth. Like many young girls, she loved sports and to be in the outdoors. Baseball and swimming in the summer and skiing in the winter were her favourites. She also loved to sing and play guitar.

The first time I saw Lizzie was downtown at a local buskerfest. There was a crowd gathered around one of the performers and I nudged my way closer to discover who the big voice belonged to. A petite girl no more than ten or eleven years old was belting out songs as she strummed a guitar almost bigger than she was. Her hair fell in wild corkscrew ringlets past her shoulders. Her sparkling eyes surveyed the audience; eyes that were an unusual grey-blue violet, like sunlight reflecting and shimmering off a frozen lake. Everyone in the crowd was tapping and clapping as they listened to an Ian Tyson song about home fries, eggs and whiskey toast. Her full volume recital held the audience captive in the palm of her wee hand.

Lizzie proved she had natural musical talent after receiving the guitar for Christmas one year. She listened to old cassette tapes belonging to her parents. Ian and Sylvia, in addition to Gordon Lightfoot, were among her favourites. Lizzie pestered her parents relentlessly until they finally agreed to let her perform at the local festival. No one listening that day would soon forget her version of "Sunshine on my Shoulders," a song made popular by John Denver back in the day. The girl with long auburn hair had swiftly stolen the show, along with my heart.

The next time I saw Lizzie, she was at a riding competition. I was volunteering at a local therapeutic riding centre, one of dozens within the province governed by OnTRA—Ontario Therapeutic Riding Association. These centres offer horseback riding as a form of therapy for children and adults with physical or cognitive impairments.

Lizzie signed up for lessons not long after she discovered she had cancer.

The news had been a shock to Lizzie and her parents. The young girl, who was never sick a day in her life, had a swollen knee that would not heal. Thoughts were she had injured it playing baseball or running, but when the pain increased to an unbearable level, there was cause for concern. Several doctors were consulted. After many tests, blood work, X-rays, and more tests, Lizzie and her parents were called in to a meeting. The news hit the family hard.

The tests showed there was a tumour in Lizzie's leg. She would need chemotherapy and an operation for a rare form of cancer called Ewing's sarcoma. Lizzie was admitted to Toronto's Hospital for Sick Children.

The next time I saw Lizzie was at a riding competition. She'd received chemotherapy but was waiting for her operation. In spite of this she had taken months of riding lessons, but this competition would be her first at the beginner level. She was weak and pale and had lost all of her beautiful, long hair. Her tiny frame was even smaller due to a loss in weight. The picture I viewed today was a complete juxtaposition from the previous summer. A wilted bloom, Lizzie was curled into the fetal position on a canvas lawn chair in the shade of a horse trailer. I tried to ignore the hurt my heart was feeling. The attempt was unsuccessful.

Lizzie was napping when the riding instructor gently woke her. It was time for her test.

"Are you up to riding?" the instructor inquired.

She blinked, her eyes no longer showing any sign of sparkle. Then she nodded and mustered strength to stand. Watching from a distance, I quietly observed nothing was going to stop this young woman from riding her beloved horse, Traveller.

Traveller was a cross between a Canadian and a Paint horse. His markings were black and white and very bold. A Canadian horse is considered a rare breed. Lizzie's choice of mount was a perfect match for her own perseverance. This was a breed known to survive against the odds.

Sharron, her mother, talked to me as Lizzie rode her test. Her tale was of endless days of treatments and long hospital stays. Sharron had quit her job to take on the task of seeing to Lizzie's care. She spoke of monitoring white blood cell counts and anti-nausea drugs: the language of cancer. She told me of Lizzie's relentless quest to keep her life as normal as possible.

The cancer surgeon's final choice had been an operation called a Van Nes rotation. Sharron described how there would be a partial amputation, which included Lizzie's knee and a portion of her thigh. Her calf would be rotated a full 180 degrees and the re-attached ankle would then become the knee joint. I listened intently to Sharron as she explained. This procedure was the best choice so that Lizzie could be fitted for a prosthetic leg.

Volunteers at the stables continued to keep up to date with regard to Lizzie's ongoing health issues. We were all worried. We all said daily prayers.

The months following the operation were a true testament to the strength of this young woman. There were ongoing series of operations. Appointments lasting hours were scheduled for the fitting of a prosthetic leg. During those months, Lizzie became a teenager. In addition to marking her birthday with balloons and a cake, Lizzie celebrated her first step without assistance.

Lizzie was offered several opportunities through the "Help a Child Smile" foundation during the course of treatments. But all she wanted was to get back on her horse. Her parents were worried it was too soon, but as always, Lizzie persisted and Lizzie won. Her riding instructor and the volunteers helped her fit in lessons between treatments, operations, and of course schoolwork.

***

And now Lizzie was riding in a regional competition. Her dressage test was part of an event including riders from several other therapeutic riding centres. The day had begun in the early morning hours at the barn. Horses' legs were carefully wrapped in long, soft polo wraps to protect them on the journey to the show in a horse trailer. After arrival at the fairground, Lizzie groomed Traveller until his coat shone. She braided his mane and then changed into her riding clothes. Tan-coloured breeches, black leather boots (custom made to accommodate her prosthetic leg), black jacket, a crisp white blouse plus a black riding helmet completed the picture of a professional equestrian.

A dressage ring is twenty metres by forty metres and has markers positioned around the arena that are visible to the rider. The markers are A, B, C, E, F, H, K and M. Markers D, X and G are not visible. X is the centre.

Once mounted on her steed, Lizzie made her way to the ring. She nodded, and the arena gate was swung open. I held my breath.

Enter the ring at a collected trot. Proceed to X. Halt and salute. Proceed at a collected trot. Track right. Shoulder-in right. Half-circle right 10 metres. Half-pass right. Proceed to H.

Lizzie knew the test by memory.

I watched her ride. Her posture and presence portrayed confidence and the maturity of one far older than that of a young girl. Her riding was a display of grace and poise associated with a seasoned equestrian.

Change rein medium trot. Collected trot. Proceed to K.

She rode like an Olympian. I thought of a quote a writer friend had shared with me recently. "Be kinder than necessary, for everyone you meet is fighting some kind of battle." Wow! If ever someone was fighting a battle, it was Lizzie. Yet she made it look easy and effortless.

She continued. Three-loop serpentine the width of the arena. Simple change of lead when crossing the centre line. Proceed to M. Medium canter. Collected canter.

The thud of Traveller's hooves as he and Lizzie passed by matched the beating of my heart.

Collected trot. Turn right. Turn right. Halt and salute. Leave arena on a free walk.

Lizzie leaned forward and patted Traveller's neck as she left the arena. The applause was loud. Lizzie glanced over and smiled at me as she rode out of the ring. I felt my heart racing as I noticed that her eyes once again were sparkling like diamonds.

It was then I felt the tears streaming down my face. Someone tapped my arm. I turned to see the man, who I had completely forgotten about, still standing at my side.

"So can you tell me now?" the man was shouting above the applause as we watched Lizzie ride off. "What's the matter with her? She looks *normal* to me."

I brushed some of the tears off my face. As I did, the smell of horse on my hand offered a calming scent.

Choose your words carefully, I thought to myself. This is important.

"Sir, she is normal. She is just like you and me." I paused to take a deep breath before continuing my reply. "Lizzie lost a leg to cancer last year." I delayed further speech to collect my thoughts. "She has overcome great obstacles in a very short period of time. Hurdles larger than anything you can imagine. I am guessing she will continue to do so." I hesitated again. "She is one the most positive influences in my life, and Lizzie is only thirteen years old."

With no more to say, I left the man standing at the side of the arena. I could see him gripping the top rail of the board fence as if to stabilize himself. His comments were blown away in the wind.

***

Abigail was waiting for my response. I steadied myself and replied. "I haven't heard anything about Lizzie in years."

She had watched my expression change and quickly replied, "*No, it's good news!* She has been cancer-free for years. She is living in New Zealand now and is one of the country's top personal trainers. And guess what? She has competed in the Winter Paralympics. Lizzie has won medals for her alpine skiing. I always knew nothing was going to stop that girl!"

So did I. Lizzie's relentless intensity was an inspiration those many years ago. I have never forgotten her determination and tenacious nature.

An unfortunate few view a disability as something wrong with the individual. How fortunate that Lizzie has always looked through the lens of life with a different perspective. She sees only endless possibility.

Many years ago a dark cloud passed by, after which sunshine broke through. I will always remember the girl who is still in my heart. I think of Lizzie riding like the wind and I remember her singing that John Denver song. Like him, I wish for a tale to make her smile and a wish for sunshine all the while.

Rev. Janet Stobie

THE GIFT

Done! I think. Well, no, but ready enough. Exhausted, I flop into bed. It's Christmas Eve. I've been preparing…forever.

Our two boys—no, young men—Isaac and Peter leave home for university next fall. They've grown up so fast. Do they really know what Christmas is about? Sigh. I hope so.

My mind slips to the pile of gaily wrapped gifts waiting under our old artificial tree. As always, I've stretched every dollar as far as I can. Several packages contain much needed underwear and socks. A grin of satisfaction spreads across my face as I picture the big lumpy green parcel, half hidden behind the tree trunk: a leather track bag for Isaac. Expensive, yes, but I bought it on sale last summer. The sports store was closing, a true bargain. He'll carry it proudly at university. Maybe he'll still have it when he starts teaching. He'll be an amazing teacher.

I roll over to cuddle up to my husband, Jack. Peter's special parcel floats into my thoughts. I can't wait to see his face when he picks that tiny box from the topmost tree branch. He'll expect a gift card, not one of my silly poems containing a clue. He's always loved my treasure hunts. Are my clues too obscure this time? I don't think so. Peter loves a challenge. When he follows the trail and finds his pro golf clubs in the closet under the stairs, he'll be so excited. He won't care that they're used. Both boys know money is tight.

I pull the covers up to my chin and force my mind to practical things. The turkey's washed and ready. What if the hydro goes off? Maybe…Let it go, I tell myself. It's nearly midnight. You can't do anything more. Go to sleep.

I snuggle down under the soft fluffy duvet, soaking in the surplus heat emanating from Jack's body. My mind slows. My body relaxes and surrenders to sleep.

Rustling sounds jerk me awake. What? "Jack…Jack…" I hiss and poke him in the ribs.

He groans.

"Someone's stealing the Christmas gifts."

"Eh…Really? Why?"

"Can't you hear them?" I squeeze his hand. "Listen."

Thump…Thud…

"Frost…wipe it off quick…"

Jack whispers into my ear. "That's just Peter. Go back to sleep."

I glance at the clock. Four a.m. More whispers from the living-room.

"It's fine. Quiet. You'll wake Mom and Dad."

My initial fear is replaced with worry. Are they just getting home? What's happened? I lie back down. A smile creeps across my face in the darkness. What are they doing? I shake myself. Go to sleep. Don't spoil their fun. I wrap my arm around Jack's warm back. He's already snoring.

Two hours later, I'm still tossing and turning. Our bedroom door bursts open. Both boys rush in, fully dressed, Cheshire cat grins lighting up their faces. Isaac shouts, "Mom, Dad, wake up! Come and see. Santa's been here. Merry Christmas."

I wrap my robe around my tired body. Jack grabs his pants and pulls them on.

"Both of you, close your eyes, and don't peek," Peter commands. He tucks my arm under his to lead me down the hall.

"Ouch!" I screech. "I've stubbed my toe on the door stop."

Peter, too excited to have sympathy, keeps right on walking. "You're okay, Mom. Come on, keep going."

The four of us shuffle into the living room.

Isaac takes command. "Okay, stop. Now, open your eyes."

A console colour television swathed in a wide scarlet ribbon and a gigantic bow, sits like a great lumbering beast, in front of the window.

I gasp. "How…?"

"Isn't it beautiful, Mom?" Peter exults. "We've been saving for months. It's used, but it works great and it's colour."

"We've been three years without a TV," Isaac adds. "When Peter and I are at university, this will entertain you and Dad. We've heard your friends groan when you know nothing about the TV shows. Now, you'll be up with the times."

Their happy faces shine with childish delight. My heart explodes with joy. They've got it. They've figured it out. They've found the magic of Christmas.

Ronald Mackay

MY PAPÁ INVITES ANGELS

As I passed her isolated cottage on my way home to la Pensión Méndez, Laurita approached me shyly, "My Papá invites angels for *Noche Buena!* You too, are invited."

Her father Miguel, like me a day-labourer in the banana plantations around Buenavista del Norte, overheard his daughter and confirmed I was indeed invited for *Noche Buena*—Christmas Eve.

A few short days later, the 24th of December 1960 duly arrived.

Miguel and Laurita were seated outside when I reached their crude cottage. Elena, Miguel's wife, emerged from the dark interior, self-consciously plump, into the light of the open doorway. All three were dressed in their Sunday best. Laurita whispered, "*El Extranjero* has come! Like us, the Foreigner wants to meet the angels!"

I still had no idea what a Roman Catholic Christmas Eve in this isolated part of Tenerife held in store. "Graven images" were distinctly absent from my dour, Scottish Presbyterian devotions. Even the fractured beauty of stained glass was suspect.

"We live modestly," Miguel said. Carrying the stools, he invited me to follow his wife and daughter inside. It was the first private home I'd entered since arriving in the Canary Islands months earlier.

"*Estas en tu casa,*" Elena offered simply. "Our home is your home."

Other than a low table and two makeshift beds, the room was devoid of furniture. Cooking and washing were conducted outside. The walls were rough-cut cinder blocks from the volcanic quarry at Taco alongside Los Silos. The Milky Way's countless millions of stars sparkled in the open doorway.

On a narrow shelf, two candles burned beneath a coloured print in a wooden frame without glass. The candlelight gave salience to its simple sanctity.

"The Virgin Mary." My plain Protestant vocabulary possessed few words for religious icons.

"*Nuestra Señora de los Remedios.*" Elena provided the precision I lacked.

"With the Baby Jesus," Laurita whispered, eyes aglow.

"It was she who liberated our country from the Moors," Elena said. "It took 700 years!"

I examined the face in her simple frame with greater respect. Nuestra Señora de los Remedios calmly returned my gaze from a more heavenly domain.

I gestured to a third unlit candle.

"That's our *ruego*, our request," Laurita whispered. Her parents exchanged private smiles.

"After the angels arrive, Papá will pray."

"Please! Sit! You are at home." Miguel gestured to a stool.

"Rice pudding with condensed milk!" Laurita could barely suppress her excitement.

Beneath the smiles of Nuestra Señora de los Remedios and the Baby Jesus, the four of us ate super-sweet rice pudding from small glass bowls. Our arms made exaggerated shadows on the unfinished walls. When we'd eaten, Miguel, with a meaningful glance at his daughter, took a wooden tray and went out into the starlight.

"Papá will now invite the angels to come in!" Laurita's dark eyes glistened.

There came three sharp raps on the door.

"Enter!" Laurita called. Miguel entered, two angels bowing on his tray.

Their bodies, six inches high, were inclined forward in respect. They were cut from the woody stalk of green *retama*, a kind of evergreen broom that grew in the volcanic soil. Twisted round the heads of the two angels were halos of coloured paper, and they wore garments made from the same material. Their "wings" were cut to shape from the delicate, filigree tips of the same plant, but dried, and had been inserted into their shoulders so convincingly that the angels appeared poised to soar.

Laurita gently took an angel in each hand and Miguel lifted her so she could place one on either side of Nuestra Señora. Done, Laurita came and sat by me. Now, in perfect unison, Elena lifted one candle, Miguel the other and held their flames under the angels' extended wings. The delicate, dried fronds flared up, then died just as swiftly leaving only glowing embers. Two puffs of gentle smoke drifted across Nuestra Señora's pale face. The smoke cleared, and sweetness filled the air.

Laurita continued to watch, entranced. Now two, singed, wingless figures bowed in reverence on either side of the Virgin and Child.

"Tell our guest what has occurred, Laurita."

"Now," Laurita explained to me, "the angels look like ordinary people. You might pass them on the path to the village without recognizing them as God's messengers. That's why we must always show respect. Anyone we meet—anyone at all—might be an angel who has sacrificed her wings to remain down here alongside us."

With Laurita and her parents, I sat contemplating the print of Nuestra Señora de los Remedios torn lovingly from a magazine. But now I knew it for what it was—an icon inspired by unadulterated faith.

"Now my Papá will light the *ruego*," Laurita whispered.

Miguel lit the third candle. All three bowed their heads to make the request. I too.

"Lighten our darkness, oh Father," Miguel asked simply. "Defend us from all perils and give us the capacity we need for the burdens ahead. Amen."

As I walked back under the stars, I marvelled at the window that I had been granted onto the transcendental, a place where souls are nourished by the glow of another world. Pausing there, alone in the moonlight with the sound of the waves that came unimpeded all the way from the Americas, I wondered at the true believer who asks for neither favours nor fortune, property nor plenty, but only for routine and refuge, for the strength necessary to work hard, live patiently, give birth safely, and show love and respect.

Laurita's Papá indeed invites angels into their lives.

Christopher Black

REVELATIONS OF THE NIGHT

Beyond the wind, beyond the seas, beyond the dawn, they went,
by land and sail, by horse, by ship, the open sky their tent,
always east they journeyed on, this caravan of eight,
two by two, or four by four, towards their common fate,
through ocean storms, through desert winds,
through hunger's grip, they passed,
and always had the same reply for those who sometimes asked,
the reasons for their travel, the meaning of their path,
to illuminate their ignorance or flee a tyrant's wrath,
'we've heard a tale of lands far-off where peace and justice reign,
it's that we've searched for far and wide but fear we search in vain,
for all we've found is misery, leavened with despair,
and among the dispossessed are few who dare
to see what's right before their eyes,
or defy with angry questions the lies that swarm like flies,'
and so they passed, in times of old, hunter, farmer, engineer,
the weaver, and the poet, with songs of woe and cheer,
the doctor and the star-man, round the world they went,
learning all they ever could, how flowers made their scent,
until one day they found a place that filled their very need,
a land where people led themselves and all had time to read,
where wars were long forgotten, for they had the best defence,
walls of wisdom, moats of tears, and arms of common sense,
where making love was still an art, and art exposed their soul,
where learning, and not riches was the only worthy goal,
and so astonished were they, at all they witnessed there,

that soon they spoke of passage home for this they had to share,
but just before the dawn appeared, in gown of rosy sky,
they all awoke from deep in sleep, and began to wonder why,
the things they'd seen were nowhere round their dying fire's light,

and wondered who would listen to revelations of the night.

Ted Amsden

THE WATCHING EYE

on the steps of an abandoned mall
a faded bankruptcy notice leads
a troupe of plastic bags
allegro…

icebergs are losing their cool!
the planet has a fever!
unholy weather blooms dominate satellite views!
    (in their centres angry fathers mouth forecasts
    of scattered furniture and broken homes)

meanwhile back of mind…creeping over yellow-caked edges
homeless worry roams amongst storage ponds

…as islands of sand sink islands of plastic arise
…capitalists target consumers but kill species
…the shadows of huge corporate maggots hover over our computer
screens

from the basement to the living room up to the bedroom and
out the window onto the roof
fear rises with steady-cam ease

the anxiety of our days?
to learn there is no flood insurance

all sweet tweets and assistance candy
governments deep in spin fantasy cannot save us
as genderless fish spawn under rec room pool tables

the payback of living silently is embedding sandbags in all new home
design

when it comes to explanation and resolve
each one of us has been left holding a bag of hot yellow planetary air

our children are so distempered they pop as they text
the soap pods pills and guns left on the side table

everywhere it's the new normal

rising water is embraced as the ultimate opportunity to share toxins
domestic waterboarding means never again looking at your home with a
dry eye
forest fire is the great equalizer as wealthy and poor learn they flee at
similar speed

it is no longer a question of when does the sun rise and set
today's calculation involves particulate density smog colour
and will I see the traffic lights as I drive between pop-up lakes?

encumbered with planetary responsibility disabled with outstanding debt
pressed inside a shrinking ecosphere   impossibility is already at
hand

return return return to a human state of trust
acting alone we come upon the foreign other
embracing the many the better versions of ourselves step forward

Untitled by Ted Amsden

Marie Arden Prins

NOVEMBER WINDOWS

A pale November sun
spotlights four windows
that frame tableaus
and buoy my heart now
chilled by days of grey
and degrees plunging
downwards towards months
of icy wind and snow.

#1
Outside the patio window,
a woodpecker hops sideways,
feet gripping rough bark,
its white breast framed
by black wing feathers,
a red cap perched on its head,
as it inches to the feeder,
hungry for suet.

#2
Beyond the kitchen window,
a dozen chickens,
buff and busy, scratch
the frosted ground strewn
with fists of frozen kale
and grain scooped from

a rusted barrel stored
beneath their stilted coop.

#3
Against a living room window,
my husband, forehead to pane,
lifts a storm and clicks it into
place beside a wavy 2 over 2,
while a pale sun silhouettes his
raised arms in an autumnal ritual
that blocks westerly winds
rising behind his back.

#4
Through an upstairs window,
a scene unfolds across the street,
as a young man nimbly climbs
the neighbour's roof to replace
crumbling bricks on a chimney
built when he erected tall
Lego towers on the carpet
next to the bed behind me.

Derek Paul

MY FIRST CONVERSATION WITH A BEAVER

During my early September absence from The Cottage on Lake Temiskaming, just north of Haileybury, the local beaver family had cut every poplar tree in sight on the property's several acres. I surveyed the damage. It was too late to save the poplars, but still I wondered, "if only I could confront the beavers!"

At dusk I had a sudden premonition that they might be coming again in search of just one more tree. There wasn't another to cut down, but beavers are optimists. So I silently slipped down to the northernmost of the beaches on the property, which I felt was their likely landing place. This beach is quite small, and is bounded by high rocks north, south and west. To my great delight, as I was still climbing down the rocks, I saw the whole beaver family swimming around the point of land north of the beach. By the time I had reached the water's edge the leader was already positioned straight out from the shore. He flapped a special signal telling the others to go home. They all turned tail at once, leaving him alone to face this giant on the shore.

By then I had picked up a stout stick and was standing, my feet apart, right arm outstretched to the top of my staff, its lower end being close to my right foot. It was an attempt at resembling Neptune, whose mythic picture I had once seen in a children's illustrated book, taking command of the waters, an image I vainly hoped to recreate in seconds. The beaver—clearly the patriarch—then began his survey. He swam slowly in a large circle, of radius about twenty yards, at the near point coming within ten yards of my position and at the far point fifty yards. Not once but twice he circled, taking many minutes to complete this whole movement. I never moved a muscle. Then he stopped at the far point and turned to face me. "Krrrriiickk," he uttered. Then again, "Krrriickk." Beaver language is a little beyond my ken. "Krrxrxriickk," I answered ungrammatically. "Krrriickk," he replied. "Krxrxrriickck," I responded incompetently. This time he didn't answer, so I repeated my krxrxrriick so as to improve upon the previous one. It must have been good enough to make him curious. He started to swim again, but now in a straight line toward me, and even slower than before. Still I never moved a muscle. He just went on coming, until at last his belly struck the pebbles six feet away from me, whereupon he gazed for some minutes on this monster that never moved but seemed to be defending his territory. Then slowly he retreated backwards, never taking his eyes off me. At twenty yards he turned for home; but I stayed on, motionless, marvelling at Creation.

Matthew King - Spirit of the Hills 2019 Poetry Contest Winner

ON THE CAMEL AT THE PETERBOROUGH ZOO AND OTHERS
(For Gobi and Wally)

There's a sign that tells you what to do
if you want to piss it off
but it looks pissed off enough already—
at least, to me it does. You can't
get over how huge it is,
or at least I can't, and when it's
lumbering at me, I back up
and I don't know how far is far enough.
Everyone says that camels spit
when they're mad—and how do you know it's mad
except that you think it's going to spit?
And it always looks about to spit,
or at least to me it does,
and it's got the size to make it count.
The size of its head!
Its enormous neck reminds you
of how you see an oak and think
how incredibly engineered it is
to hold all that weight by just one joint—
or at least I do, and if you don't
just think of some guy you've seen explaining
torture techniques, who said
"try holding your arm straight out ten minutes!"

Well, try it. I'll wait.
…you get the idea and so
you see why this camel might be mad
about holding its head up all day long—
and kids keep on riding up and down
on bicycles, like the sign suggests.
This camel to me is something wholly other,
not comprehended like the pig
that nibbles your fingers out of cheerful
domestication, or the snakes
and lizards and monkeys in their glass
containers, displayed like on a screen.
But then when I turn to go
I turn from its slobbering mouth and
its threatening stare, I turn to the side,
to its singular eye, and enter in,
not facing but seen and seeing,
nothing to do with confrontation,
nothing to do with recognition,
nothing to do with self and other
just taking it in
and we are the same

and the day before he died
Wally on drugs, his pupils deep as space
looked into my eyes as if
he couldn't believe we never saw
what we saw before

Felicity Sidnell Reid

RED FOX AND DEER

A red fox springs out of grey winter bush,
a bronze coat his armour in thorny drifts.
Dark eyes knowing, he parades his charms.
Waving his black-tipped bushy tail,
he runs along the icy foot path
round the marsh, blue crinkled under
sudden, winter sun. Performance over
he retires into a hidden solitude.
Then three does cross my path,
unworried by my presence, taking their time.
After all, they can vanish in one leap,
their coats blending with the shadowy trees.
But they stop among the moss and fallen
timber, turning their heads in enquiry.
What am I doing in their space?
Can we share this wilderness? Perhaps,
but their questing eyes are checking me.
I bow my head and walk away,
and invisible birds sing a harmony.

Kim Aubrey

STILL HOLDING

Fierce winds have flattened swathes
of beach, adhered sand with ice.
Everything shrinks into itself.

Even the logs have moved further
up shore, stretched like sleeping hobos
letting go into earth's slow decay.

But grass still holds green, tree tips fly
their yellow-brown flags, dulled now
like the pink roses frozen to their stems.

And sun still warms me as it bleaches a path
across waves. Eyes drink in light to guard
against the deepening November dark,

to shore me up like the retaining wall,
rocks encased in brilliant ice. This time
of year I learn to absorb, not deflect,

like the two cars that meet by the boardwalk,
windows down, faces turned towards and away
from one another in earnest daily communion.

Untitled by Katalin Futo

Felicity Sidnell Reid

CARETAKING OR TAKING CARE?

Last year…leaves fell
then snow, floating, falling
dancing, in a world beyond
closed windows.

Taking care eased winter
days but chasms opened,
when spring budded through
wide windows.

A room, a bed, pictures on the wall.
And, for a while, drives in
summer countryside, ice-cream
outings, but they ended.

Guilt and grief pursue me
over smouldering hills, as fall
withers us into frailty, turns
the world spectral.

Hard to reconcile love with
deliverance of one's love
to others' care—only our
entwined fingers remain.

And now as winter snaps
its bitter jaws, a final illness,
carries him away—peacefully,
but leaves me grieving in the cold.

Christopher Cameron

A PROMISE MADE

Soft chords reverberate through the organ pipes and fill the air around me. In my chest I can feel the gentle vibrations of the bass notes. I am standing in the chancel of a large church, surrounded by flowers, looking out over the assembled congregation; the faces of some of my oldest friends are looking back up at me. I take a breath and sing the first words, barely audibly with reverent slowness, as the composer wished.

"Our Father…"

I am singing at the funeral of the mother of an old friend, and I shouldn't be here doing this. The last time I sang *The Lord's Prayer* by Albert Hay Malotte was decades ago. In the last five years I have not sung a note.

The piece begins quietly and reflectively but will swell at the end to a powerful conclusion. In my best days I used to draw tears from brides when I sang the quiet parts and shake the beams of churches with my crescendo. Today I promise myself that I will be happy just to get to the end of the piece.

***

I began singing when I was a teenager, as easily and naturally as a flock of birds taking flight. Someone told me I was good at it, which came as a happy surprise because I liked doing it. It was like falling in love with someone who also happened to love me. I spent several decades as a professional opera singer, never truly believing my good fortune at being able to do what I did.

I loved the primal sensuality of singing: controlling the music as it welled up from inside me and rose through my body like laughter or tears. I loved to feel it flying from me in waves of breath and reverberation, flowing outward to wash over the stage, the lights, the audience itself. Most of all, I loved the power of my voice as it travelled up the ribbons of light shining on me and then echoed off the walls of the theatre, coming back to me at the speed of sound.

***

I started to lose my hearing in my early fifties, beginning with high frequencies. I remember noticing that I couldn't hear crickets singing on a late summer night. At first it was an inconvenience, an embarrassment—someone always had to tell me when my watch alarm was going off. Conversations in groups sank into a kind of burbling mire of sound. I got very good at nodding and smiling, pretending I could follow what was going on and inferring what was being said by guesswork. The technique failed often: I once held a detailed conversation about Sudbury with a woman who told me that she and her husband were going there. Months later, I learned she had actually said that she and her husband were going to separate.

When I was singing on the stage, the music from the voices around me developed a sort of tinny, splintered quality. The sounds grew thin and distant, as if I were standing apart from everyone else. But having trouble hearing the others was not what frightened me.

I was having trouble hearing myself.

At first I thought I was losing my voice. I was doing everything the way I always had; I could feel it, I just didn't seem to be making any noise. I began to "push," a singer's term for forcing the sound, which can result in tuning and control problems. I felt as if my voice was being torn from me bit by bit, to the point where it sounded about as resonant to my ears as a rasp file being dragged down a block of wood. It was like inhabiting someone else's body—someone who couldn't sing.

I searched for a cause, but the literature is sparse on the role that hearing loss plays among classical singers. I learned that my type is called sensorineural, which simply means that it is related to the cranial nerve or the inner ear. An audiologist told me that most people lose some hearing as they age; I was just losing mine earlier and more severely. Hearing aids were prescribed.

Compared to people with profound deafness, my situation is not a tale of struggle and pain. My hearing loss is not completely disabling in the normal world: I can hear low frequencies well, and when I'm wearing my hearing aids I can glean enough words to function in most one-on-one situations. But the frequencies at which my hearing is weakest are precisely those at which my singing voice resonates, and nothing helps much with this.

***

My friend Les and I have known each other since we were teenagers. His mother was a robust supporter of all us singers when we were growing up. She came to our concerts, fed us, and gossiped with us when we were at her house; she loved to think of us as part of her extended family.

Sometime in the 1980s, when I was having some modest success singing for a living, she declared to me in her stout Nova Scotia tones that I must sing at her funeral when it came along. At the time it wasn't difficult for me to promise—half-seriously—to be on call in case she decided to shuffle off anytime soon.

I lost touch with Les over the years, although I got news of him from time to time. He became a respected high school music teacher, a beloved mentor of young instrumentalists. I had not heard from him for a long time until he called recently to say that his mother had died at the age of 95, and to ask me if I remembered the promise I'd made three decades earlier.

"God, Chris, she loved your voice so much," said Les.

A promise made is a debt unpaid, as Robert Service wrote, and despite everything it never occurred to me to turn him down. I jokingly agreed to do anything he asked for, as long as it had a range of no more than five notes and lasted no longer than four bars. But I knew she would have wanted the Lord's Prayer, so that is what I offered to sing.

There followed a concerted effort to find the sheet music, buried somewhere in my house and lost since before my children were born. I didn't really need the music—I could easily have sung it from memory; but I wanted to have my own copy, the one I had used at countless weddings and funerals all those years ago. I thought that holding in my hands this dog-eared, faded link to my past life would somehow help me.

***

Dame Evelyn Glennie, a world-renowned percussionist, has written that hearing is just a specialized form of touch. She has described an ideal state of instrumental performance where the musical sound is born beneath the surface of the instrument, guided and nurtured by the player on its journey from a place in time and space even *before* it begins to be heard. She knows what she's talking about: Evelyn Glennie happens to be profoundly deaf.

To me, her explanation perfectly illustrates the natural production of a singing voice. It can begin as nothing else but a feeling, a sense; it can come from nowhere else but deep inside my body.

But once the sound has been created within me, I need to hear it in the air to use it. To me, singing is an endless loop of vocalizing, listening, evaluating, and adjusting. And this is what I cannot do. Singing without hearing myself feels like writing with the wrong hand or walking down the street backwards: technically achievable, but alien and frustrating, impossible to do as well as I want or need.

Several years ago I stopped performing altogether.

It brings up an existential question. What kind of musician was I that I was able to walk away from my art so completely after investing so much of my life in it? Should I not have raged against the dying of the sound and found a way to keep singing? Long after he had lost all his hearing, Beethoven sat on the floor and hammered away at a legless piano so he could try to capture the vibrations. Evelyn Glennie performs barefoot so she can feel the music travelling up her body. Is it right that I no longer sing just because it isn't as easy as it used to be? Because it isn't as much fun? Maybe I should have kept hammering. Maybe I should have fought harder.

***

I am worried everyone in the congregation today is expecting something more than what I can share with them. They are waiting for the performer I once was and I know I will be less than that. But I also know that the sound of my voice doesn't belong to me today; it belongs to the people sitting in the church, to my old friends, and to the woman who asked me over thirty years ago to sing at her funeral. My voice will resonate everywhere but in my own ears. I will make the sounds, and everyone else will do the hearing: a perfect communion of performer and listener.

While the organ plays the short introduction—music I sense more than hear—a feeling comes over me that I have not been expecting. One of the things I used to love about performing was the sensation of being swept along by a force that was greater than I was. I would feel like a diver who has just left the board, poised between the reality of the past and the quantum possibilities of the future; a musician in music that was both familiar and mysterious. I have not felt this in years, but I am feeling it now as I take my breath to sing the first words.

"Our Father..."

A powerful calm fills me. I clear my mind and allow my body to control the resonance I pray is reaching the ears of the listeners. As they always have, the notes lift off the page I am holding and rise through me. I become the music's instrument, creating the sound inside and shaping the composer's words with my mouth. Near the climax, the organ draws me into a vortex of sound as all the stops are pulled. I know my voice must be echoing off the faraway walls of the church. The power and the glory forever.

The final vocal challenge is a diminuendo to soften the final note— the Amen—from fortissimo to pianissimo over several bars, and to let it

208

die away into the air. I can only do this by feel, but inside my head the feeling seems flawless. I am done; for now or forever, I can't say. I lift my eyes to the vaulted ceiling where I know my voice has been ringing seconds before, exhale slowly, and close the music.

-End-

CONTRIBUTORS

Ted Amsden has several obsessions: writing, photography, motorcycling and following the news. He is the Poet Laureate Emeritus of Cobourg.

Kim Aubrey's stories, essays, and poems have appeared in journals and anthologies including *Best Canadian Stories, Event, Numero Cinq, Room* and *The New Quarterly*. Her story collection, *What We Hold in Our Hands*, won an Honourable Mention in the Bermuda Literary Awards. Kim leads an annual writers' retreat in Bermuda.

Lynn C. Bilton moved to Northumberland County in the fall of 2017. She has recently discovered the *fun* of writing. "Grand Skating," her first published short story, was a submission chosen to be included in *Place Settings—Collected Works Celebrating the County of Brant*.

Christopher Black is a traveller through time, a student of life, a lawyer, an actor, a poet, guitarist, author of the novel, *Beneath the Clouds*, and numerous essays on legal-political themes in a number of international journals.

Alan Bland is a saxophonist, photographer, kayaker, cook and writer who has had several of his short stories published while hoping to unleash some of his longer fiction on an unsuspecting public. Meantime he writes legal opinions as an expert witness for trials at the Ontario Superior Court.

Christopher Cameron enjoyed a successful career as a professional opera singer, retiring in 2009. Several years ago he began a new career as a freelance writer and editor. His first book, a memoir of his singing years, *Dr. Bartolo's Umbrella and Other Tales from my Surprising Operatic Life*, was published in 2017. In June 2017 Chris and his wife Karen moved from Toronto to the banks of the Trent River in Campbellford.

Michael Croucher, a novelist and award-winning short story writer lives with his wife in Cobourg. They have two married daughters and five grandchildren. A former Toronto Police detective, Mike writes crime, mystery and general fiction. He has published two novels: *Bravo's Veil* and *Diamond Run*.

Antony Di Nardo is the award-winning author of four collections of poetry, his most recent, *Skylight*, released in 2018. His work appears in anthologies and journals across Canada and internationally. He divides his time between Cobourg, Ontario and Sutton, Quebec.

Esther Sokolov Fine York University Professor Emerita/Senior Scholar, graduated University of Michigan, doctorate from OISE, MFA from Vermont College of Fine Arts. Received Hopwood Award for fiction and Educational Press Association of America Distinguished Achievement Award. Recent publications include: *Raising Peacemakers* (Garn Press) and *Playing the Bully* (chapter book with J. Head, V. Shearham).

Katalin Futo is a retired structural engineer with a lifelong interest in the visual arts. She returned to the visual arts after early retirement eight years ago and took evening classes and workshops in drawing and oil painting. After moving to Cobourg she joined the Cobourg Art Club. She aims for poetic realism in drawings and paintings and truly enjoys the moment when a drawing or painting suddenly comes alive.

Kim Grove has been published in the *Globe and Mail*, *The Christian Science Monitor*, *The Toronto Star* and various smaller publications. She has taught writing at Loyalist College, the Trenton Air Force Base, the Colborne Community Care Centre and Ciego de Avila University in Cuba. Her teaching comes from a love of reading what others have to share.

Richard Marvin Grove, known to friends as Tai, 1953, Hamilton born, lives in Presqu'ile Provincial Park in Ontario, where he and his wife, Kim, run a B&B. He is a photographer, writer, editor, and publisher. His art and photographs are in over 30 corporate collections across Canada. He has 16 book titles to his name and his images have been used as cover art for more than 40 books. Find his B&B at: www.hiddenbrookpress.com/hbp-artists-retreat. Find his Writer's Blog at: https://richardgrovewriter.wordpress.com/

Carolyn Helfenstein's fascination with writing and storytelling blossomed with each career that included teaching in a one-room school (age 17-18), co-owning and operating an award-winning dairy farm (25 years) and an award-winning newspaper (12 years). *Why Not?* her first published book, released in 2008 was followed by *Rock Solid*, a Newfoundland saga released in 2018.

Linda Hutsell-Manning has eleven published children's books as well as short fiction and poetry in literary magazines. Her latest novel is *That Summer in Franklin* (Second Story Press). A two-act comedy, "A Certain Singing Teacher" was premiered in 2017. "Finding Moufette" was published online by Common Deer Press in 2018 and her memoir, *Fearless and Determined: Two Years Teaching in a One-Room School*, will be published by Blue Denim Press in October 2019.

Shane Joseph is a novelist, blogger, reviewer, short story writer, travel agent and publisher living in Cobourg. His latest novel, *Milltown*, was released in April 2019. For details, visit his website at www.shanejoseph.com.

Wally Keeler, aka Poetician1, is founder and director of the Imagine Nation of the Peoples Republic of Poetry. Wally has published in literary/art journals in Canada and abroad, as well as performances and exhibitions in assorted media. Wally is adept at the fusion of poetry with photo and video.

Matthew King taught philosophy for some years at York University. He now tries to grow things near Marmora, Ontario, and canoes around Wollaston Lake, and takes pictures of birds and bugs, and hopes to speak the mystery of the lighting of being.

Georgeina Knapp has been writing short stories since she was a child. Recently she helped write the history of the village church she has attended since 1957, and *Living the Dream* was published this year. She's never won a writing competition and is overjoyed to see her winning entry published in *Hill Spirits IV*.

Margaret Kropf is a local poet who has been published in several Canadian literary journals. She has also acted in local theatre and participates in storytelling, especially French Canadian folk tales. She is an active participant in Toastmasters International.

Dania Madera -Lerman's passion for art began when drawing in the sand on the shores of Georgian Bay. Her painting is characterized by bold, structured, yet free-flowing lines and vibrant colour. Inspired by a variety of painters, she is also influenced by her 20 years teaching persons of different ages and abilities and watching them discover art's beauty.

Dania has won many awards and is the subject of two TV documentaries. Her work is collected internationally by both public and private sectors. http://www.daniaspaintings.com

Ronald Mackay has farmed, taught, and managed international development projects. A public speaker, Ronald writes drama, memoir and fiction. *Fortunate Isle, a Memoir of Tenerife* captures life in a small village in the Canary Islands in the 1960s. He and his wife live near Keene, Ontario.

Maureen Mullally is an artist who writes. Having caught the bug from her late husband, Brian, she writes when she is not painting.

Reva Nelson is a former professional actress, teacher-librarian, workshop leader and keynote speaker. She moved to Cobourg from Toronto three years ago and now volunteers at the Art Gallery of Northumberland and on two boards. Reva writes for local publications and has recently relaunched the coaching and facilitation part of her business. Contact her at www.revanelson.ca

Jessica Outram's play *Once Upon a Rocking Chair* recently had a run of sold out performances in Cobourg. *The Writing Spiral* is about eight thematic spirals exploring how to cultivate a writing life. *From the Cottage Porch* captures the spirit of cottage life. Jessica is a member of the Playwrights Guild of Canada and blogs at www.sunshineinajar.com

Derek Paul is a retired physicist, a generalist and board member of Coalition Climat Montréal. He has edited numerous books and, in addition to his many articles, has published *Chin*, a fable, *Love's Labours Regained*, a play in four acts and, non-fiction, *A Leap to an Ecological Economy*.

Marie Arden Prins is a remedial reading teacher with her own practice, The Reading Room. She lives with her artist husband in an historic, octagonal home in Colborne. She writes memoir pieces, poetry, and children's books, including a mid-grade novel *The Girl from the Attic* soon to be published by Common Deer Press. Much of her work is inspired by the history of her home and its surrounding gardens. www.marieprins.ca

Felicity Sidnell Reid is co-author of books for teachers and students. Her poetry has been anthologized in print and online journals. Her novel, *Alone: A Winter in the Woods* published by Hidden Brook Press is to be released as an e-book in 2019. Felicity is the co-host of Word on the Hills, a literary radio series now in its sixth year. Visit her at felicitysidnellreid.com

Cynthia Reyes's published writing includes 4 books and several short stories in a variety of genres. Her new *Myrtle the Purple Turtle* children's books have been critically acclaimed bestsellers. A former writer-director, executive producer and journalism trainer with CBC Television, Cynthia produced more than a hundred episodes of network TV programs. National and international awards include the Diamond Book Award for Book of the Year, the Children's Broadcast Institute Award, The Trailblazer Award, and the Crystal Award for Outstanding Achievement in Film and Television.

James Ronson, a lifelong writer, published his first novel, *Power and Possessions*, in the spring of 2015. "Deep Dive" is a memoir about a scary moment he experienced while diving off the barrier reef in Cozumel, Mexico. His second novel, *Blood, Fire and Ice*, will be published in the fall of 2019.

Gwynn Scheltema has been a columnist, freelancer and a fiction editor for *Lichen Arts & Letters Preview*. Her award-winning fiction and poetry have appeared in literary magazines and anthologies. She produces and co-hosts Word on the Hills radio show on Northumberland 89.7 FM, and writes, edits, coaches and teaches creative writing through www.writescape.ca.

René Schmidt worked at many dirty and dangerous jobs before enrolling in York University's Creative Writing Program and Faculty of Education. His four books on *Canadian Disasters* by Scholastic Canada have all sold well. His novel, *Leaving Fletchville* won the O.L.A. Red Maple Honour Award as voted by student readers. He is happily married and lives in Trenton.

Susan Statham, a graduate of Algonquin College and the University of Waterloo, is the author of *The Painter's Craft* and winner of the Medli Award for *True Image*. She is an editor and contributor to *Hill Spirits I, II, III, & IV*. Susan is the current president of Spirit of the Hills Arts Association.

Rev. Janet Stobie is a writer, storyteller, and ordained minister. She served nineteen years in parish ministry. She has written two novels, two short story collections, three children's books, and a worship resource. Janet writes a column for the *Millbrook Times* and a blog titled "Tips for Grace-filled Living." Sample her books and her blog at www.janetstobie.com

Diane Taylor is the author of *From the Heart of the Ship* and *The Gift of Memoir*. She has published non-fiction stories in *Canadian Yachting*, the *Journal of Palliative Care, Ontario Out of Doors*, and others. For twenty years, she has been giving workshops in memoir writing. Visit dianemtaylor.com for more information.

Michael Topa was born in Michigan, and grew up there and in Texas and Afghanistan. He has been writing poetry for more than 50 years and has published poems in small magazines in the United States and Canada. In 2017, Michael self-published a volume of poetry, titled *Unfinished Business*.

Donna Wootton has a new novel from Hidden Brook Press called *What Shirley Missed*. Recently she has been happy writing poetry and blogs. Her nonfiction writing includes a book about her late father called *Moon Remembered*. Please visit her at www.dmwootton.com.